Anti-Slavery Opinions

BEFORE THE YEAR 1800

READ BEFORE THE CINCINNATI LITERARY CLUB, NOVEMBER 16, 1872

By WILLIAM FREDERICK POOLE

Librarian of the Public Library of Cincinnati

To which is appended a fac simile Reprint of Dr. George Buchanan's Oration on the Moral and Political Evil of Slavery, delivered at a public meeting of the Maryland Society for Promoting the Abolition of Slavery, Baltimore, July 4, 1791

CINCINNATI
ROBERT CLARKE & CO.
1873

ANTI-SLAVERY OPINIONS

Before 1800.

I purpose this evening to call the attention of the Club to the state of anti-slavery opinions in this country just prior to the year 1800. In this examination I shall make use of a very rare pamphlet in the library of General Washington, which seems to have escaped the notice of writers on this subject; and shall preface my remarks on the main topic of discussion with a brief description of the Washington collection.

In the library of the Boston Athenæum, the visitor sees, as he enters, a somewhat elaborately-constructed book-case, with glass front, filled with old books. This is the library of George Washington, which came into possession of the Athenæum in 1849. It was purchased that year from the heirs of Judge Bushrod Washington —the favorite nephew to whom the General left all his books and manuscripts—by Mr. Henry Stevens, of London, with the intention of placing it in the British Museum. Before the books were shipped, they were bought by Mr. George Livermore and a few other literary and public-spirited gentlemen of Boston, and presented to the Athenæum. Mr. Livermore, as discretionary executor of the estate of Thomas Dowse, the "literary leather-dresser" of Cambridge, added to the gift one thousand dollars, for the purpose of printing a description and catalogue of the collection, which has not yet been done.

The collection numbers about twelve hundred titles, of which four hundred and fifty are bound volumes, and seven hundred and fifty are pamphlets and unbound serials. Some books of the original library of General Washington still remain at Mt. Vernon, and are, or were a few years since, shown to visitors, with other curiosities.

Separated from association with their former illustrious owner, the bound volumes, which are mostly English books, present but few attractions. Among them are a few treatises on the art of war and military tactics, which evidently were never much read. These were imported after his unfortunate expedition with Braddock's army, and before the revolutionary war. There are books on horse and cattle diseases; on domestic medicine; on farming, and on religious topics—such works as we might expect to find on the shelves of an intelligent Virginia planter. It is evident that their owner was no student or specialist. Many of the books were sent to him as presents, with complimentary inscriptions by the donors. The bindings are all in their original condition, and generally of the most common description. The few exceptions were presentation copies.

Col. David Humphreys, Washington's aid-de-camp during the revolutionary war, presents his "Miscellaneous Works," printed in 1790, bound, regardless of expense, by some Philadelphia binder, in full red morocco, gilt and goffered edges, and with covers and fly-leaves lined with figured satin. As the book was for a very distinguished man, the patriotic binder has stamped on the covers and back every device he had in his shop. Nearly all the volumes have the bold autograph of "G? Washington," upon their title pages, and the well-known book-plate, with his name, armorial bearings, and motto, *Exitus acta probat*,* on the inside of the covers.

There are persons at the present day who have very positive opinions on the subject of prose fiction, believing that great characters like Jonathan Edwards and George Washington never read such naughty books when they were young. Let us see. Here is the "Adventures of Peregrine Pickle; in which are included the Memoirs of a Lady of Quality," by Tobias Smollett, in three volumes. On the title page of the first volume is the autograph of George Washington, written in the

---

* The questionable morality of Gen. Washington's motto might suggest that it was not originally adopted by him. The sentiment, that "the end justifies the means," has been charged, as a reproach, upon the Jesuits. It was the motto of the Northamptonshire family from which Gen. Washington descended, and was used by him, probably without a thought of its Jesuitical association, or its meaning.

cramped hand of a boy of fourteen. The work shows more evidence of having been attentively read, even to the end of the third volume, than any in the library. Here is the " Life and Opinions of John Buncle," a book which it is better that boarding-school misses should not read. Yet Washington read it, and enjoyed the fun; for it is one of the few books he speaks of in his correspondence as having read and enjoyed. The present generation of readers are not familiar with John Buncle. Of the book and its author, Hazlitt says: "John Buncle is the English Rabelais. The soul of Francis Rabelais passed into Thomas Amory, the author of John Buncle. Both were physicians, and enemies of much gravity. Their great business was to enjoy life. Rabelais indulges his spirit of sensuality in wine, in dried neats' tongues, in Bologna sausages, in Botorgas. John Buncle shows the same symptoms of inordinate satisfaction in bread and butter. While Rabelais roared with Friar John and the monks, John Buncle gossiped with the ladies."

It is the good fortune of the youth of our age that they are served with fun in more refined and discreet methods; yet there is a melancholy satisfaction in finding in the life of a great historical character like Washington, who was the embodiment of dignity and propriety, that he could, at some period of his existence, unbend and enjoy a book like John Buncle. He becomes, thereby, more human; and the distance between him and ordinary mortals seems to diminish.

Thomas Comber's "Discourses on the Common Prayer," has three autographs of his father, Augustine Washington, one of his mother, Mary Washington, and one of his own, written when nine years of age. The fly-leaves he had used as a practice book for writing his father's and mother's names and his own, and for constructing monograms of the family names.*

The pamphlets in the collection have intrinsically more value than the larger works. They were nearly all contemporaneous, and were sent to Washington by

---

* On one of the fly-leaves, written in a boy's hand, is " Mary Washington and George Washington." Beneath is this memorandum: " The above is in General Washington's handwriting when nine years of age. [Signed,] G. W. Parke Custis," who was the grandson of Mrs. Washington, and the last surviver of the family. He was born in 1781, and died at the Arlington House in 1857.

In the appraisement of General Washington's estate, after his death, this book was valued at twenty-five cents, and the Miscellaneous Works of Col. Humphreys, at three dollars. The boy's scribbling, in the one case, and the gorgeous binding in the other, probably determined these values. In the appendix of Mr. Everett's Life of Washington, is printed the appraisers' inventory of Washington's library. Tracts on Slavery was valued at $1.00; Life of John Buncle, 2 vols., $3.00; Peregrine Pickle, 3 vols., $1.50; Humphrey Clinker, 25c.; Jefferson's Notes on Virginia, $1.50; Tom Jones, or the History of a Foundling, 3 vols., (third vol. wanting) $1.50; Gulliver's Travels, 2 vols., 1.50; Pike's Arithmetic, $2.00,

their authors, with inscriptions upon the title pages in their authors' handwriting, of the most profound respect and esteem. Some of these pamphlets are now exceedingly rare. In a bound volume lettered "Tracts on Slavery," and containing several papers, all of radical anti-slavery tendencies,* is the one to which I wish especially to call your attention. It is so rare that, having shown this copy for fifteen years to persons especially interested in this subject, and having made the most diligent inquiry, I have never heard of another, till within a few days since, when I learn from my friend, Mr. George H. Moore, the librarian of the New York Historical Society, that there is a copy in that society's

---

*The first of these tracts is "A Serious Address to the Rulers of America, on the Inconsistency of their Conduct respecting Slavery; forming a contrast between the encroachments of England on American liberty, and American injustice in tolerating slavery. By a Farmer, London," 1783. 24 pages. 8vo. The author compared, in opposite columns, the speeches and resolutions of the members of Congress in behalf of their own liberty, with their conduct in continuing the slavery of others. I have never seen the name of the author of this tract. It was extensively circulated at the time, and had much influence in forming the anti-slavery sentiment which later existed. Another is "An Essay on the Impolicy of the African Slave Trade. In two Parts. By the Rev. T. Clarkson, M. A. To which is added an Oration upon the Necessity of Establishing at Paris a Society for Promoting the Abolition of the Trade and Slavery of the Negroes. By J. P. Brissot de Warville. Philadelphia: Printed by Francis Bailey, for 'the Pennsylvania Society for Promoting the Abolition of Slavery, and the Relief of Free Negroes unlawfully held in Bondage.' 1789." 155 pp. 8vo.

library. Its title is: "An Oration upon the Moral and Political Evil of Slavery. Delivered at a Public Meeting of the Maryland Society for Promoting the Abolition of Slavery and the Relief of Free Negroes and others unlawfully held in Bondage, Baltimore, July 4, 1791. By George Buchanan, M. D., Member of the American Philosophical Society. Baltimore: Printed by Philip Edwards, M,DCC,XCIII." Twenty pages, octavo.

A Fourth-of-July oration in Baltimore, on the moral and political evils of slavery, only four years after the adoption of the Constitution, is an incident worthy of historical recognition, and a place in anti-slavery literature. The following extracts will give an idea of its style and range of thought:

"God hath created mankind after His own image, and granted them liberty and independence; and if varieties may be found in their structure and color, these are only to be attributed to the nature of their diet and habits, as also to the soil and the climate they may inhabit, and serve as flimsy pretexts for enslaving them.

"What, will you not consider that the Africans are men? That they have human souls to be saved? That they are born free and independent? A violation of these prerogatives is an infringement upon the laws of God.

"Possessed of Christian sentiments, they fail not to exercise them when opportunity offers. Things pleasing rejoice them, and melancholy circumstances pall their appetites for amusements. They brook no insults, and are equally prone to forgiveness, as to resentments. They have gratitude also, and will even expose their lives to wipe off the obligation of past favors; nor do they want any of the refinements of taste, so much the boast of those who call themselves Christians.

"The talent for music, both vocal and instrumental, appears natural to them; neither is their genius for literature to be despised. Many instances are recorded of men of eminence among them. Witness Ignatius Sancho, whose letters are admired by all men of taste. Phillis Wheatley, who distinguished herself as a poetess; the Physician of New Orleans; the Virginia Calculator; Banneker, the Maryland Astronomer, and many others, whom it would be needless to mention. These are sufficient to show, that the Africans whom you despise, whom you inhumanly treat as brutes, and whom you unlawfully subject to slavery, are equally capable of improvement with yourselves.

"This you may think a bold assertion; but it is not made without reflection, nor independent of the testimony of many who have taken pains in their education. Because you see few, in comparison to their number, who make any exertion of ability at all, you are ready to enjoy the common opinion that they are an inferior set of beings, and destined to the cruelties and hardships you impose upon them.

"But be cautious how long you hold such sentiments; the time may come when you will be obliged to abandon them. Consider the pitiable situation of these most distressed beings, deprived of their liberty and reduced to slavery. Consider also that they toil not for themselves from the rising of the sun to its going down, and you will readily conceive the cause of their inaction. What time or what incitement has a slave to become wise? There is no great art in hilling corn, or in running a furrow; and to do this they know they are doomed, whether they seek into the mysteries of science or remain ignorant as they are.

"To deprive a man of his liberty has a tendency to rob his soul of every spring to virtuous actions; and were slaves to become fiends, the wonder could not be great. 'Nothing more assimilates a man to a beast,' says the learned Montesquieu, 'than being among freemen, himself a slave; for slavery clogs the mind, perverts the moral faculty, and reduces the conduct of man to the standard of brutes.' What right have you to expect greater things of these poor mortals? You would not blame a brute for committing ravages upon his prey; nor ought you to censure a slave for making attempts to regain his liberty, even at the risk of life itself.

"Such are the effects of subjecting man to slavery,

that it destroys every human principle, vitiates the mind, instills ideas of unlawful cruelties, and subverts the springs of government.

"What a distressing scene is here before us? America, I start at your situation! These direful effects of slavery demand your most serious attention. What! shall a people who flew to arms with the valor of Roman citizens when encroachments were made upon their liberties by the invasion of foreign powers, now basely descend to cherish the seed and propagate the growth of the evil which they boldly sought to eradicate? To the eternal infamy of our country this will be handed down to posterity, written in the blood of African innocence. If your forefathers have been degenerate enough to introduce slavery into your country to contaminate the minds of her citizens, you ought to have the virtue of extirpating it.

"In the first struggles for American freedom, in the enthusiastic ardor of attaining liberty and independence, one of the most noble sentiments that ever adorned the human breast was loudly proclaimed in all her councils. Deeply penetrated with the sense of equality, they held it as a fixed principle, 'that all men are by nature, and of right ought to be, free; that they were created equal, and endowed by their Creator with certain inalienable rights, among which are life, liberty, and the pursuit of happiness. Nevertheless, *when* the blessings of peace were showered upon them; *when* they had obtained these rights which they had so boldly contended for, *then* they became apostates to their principles, and riveted the fetters of slavery upon the unfortunate Africans.

"Deceitful men! Who could have suggested that American patriotism would at this day countenance a conduct so inconsistent; that while America boasts of being a land of freedom, and an asylum for the oppressed of Europe, she should at the same time foster an abominable nursery of slaves to check the shoots of her growing liberty? Deaf to the clamors of criticism, she feels no remorse, and blindly pursues the object of her destruction; she encourages the propagation of vice, and suffers her youth to be reared in the habits of cruelty. Not even the sobs and groans of injured innocence which reek from every state can excite her pity, nor human misery bend her heart to sympathy. Cruel and oppressive she wantonly abuses the rights of man, and willingly sacrifices her liberty upon the altar of slavery.

"What an opportunity is here given for triumph among her enemies! Will they not exclaim that, upon this very day, while the Americans celebrate the anniversary of freedom and independence, abject slavery exists in all her states but one? [Note—Massachusetts.] How degenerately base to merit the rebuke! Fellow countrymen, let the heart of humanity awake and direct your councils. Combine to drive the fiend monster from your territories.

"Your laborers are slaves, and they have no incentive to be industrious; they are clothed and victualed, whether lazy or hard-working; and, from the calculations that have been made, one freeman is worth two slaves in the field, which make it in many instances cheaper to have hirelings; for they are incited to industry by hopes of reputation and future employment, and are careful of their apparel and their implements of husbandry, where they must provide them for themselves; whereas the others have little or no temptation to attend to any of these circumstances.

"Fellow countrymen, let the hand of persecution be no longer raised against you; act virtuously; 'do unto all men as you would that they should do unto you,' and exterminate the pest of slavery from the land."

The orator then goes on to hold up the horrors of an insurrection. He reminds his hearers that in many parts of the South the number of slaves exceeds that of the whites. He reminds them that these slaves are naturally born free and have a right to freedom; that they will not forever sweat under the yoke of slavery. "Heaven," he says, "will not overlook such enormities. She is bound to punish impenitent sinners, and her wrath is to be dreaded by all. What, then, if the fire of liberty shall be kindled among them? What if some enthusiast in their cause shall beat to arms and call them to the standard of freedom? Led on by the hopes of freedom and animated by the inspiring voice of their leaders, they would soon find that 'a day, an hour of virtuous liberty was worth a whole eternity of bondage.'

"Hark! methinks I hear the work begun; the blacks have sought for allies and have found them in the wilderness, and have called the rusty savages to their assistance, and are preparing to take revenge upon their haughty masters."

To this threatening passage the orator has appended a note, in which he says: "This was thrown out as a conjecture of what possibly might happen; and the insurrections of San Domingo tend to prove this danger to be more considerable than has generally been supposed, and sufficient to alarm the inhabitants of these states."

The contingency, which he thought might possibly happen, did actually occur thirty-nine years later, when an insurrection broke out, August, 1830, in Southampton county, Virginia, under the lead of Nat Turner, a fanatical negro preacher, in which sixty-one white men, women, and children were murdered before it was suppressed.

He recommends immediate emancipation; and if this can not be done, "then," he says, "let the children be liberated at a certain age, and in less than half a century the plague will be totally rooted out from among you; thousands of good citizens will be added to your number, and gratitude will induce them to become your friends."

This remarkable oration suggests some interesting questions of historical inquiry. How far do these opinions represent the current sentiments of that time on the subject of slavery? It will be seen that they are of the most radical type. I am not aware that Wendell Phillips or Wm. Lloyd Garrison ever claimed that the negro race was equal in its capacity for improvement to the white race. While their rhetoric was more chaste, they certainly never denounced the system in more vigorous and condemnatory terms.

Forty-four years later (October 21, 1835), Mr. Garrison was waited upon, in open day, by a mob of most respectable citizens, while attending a meeting of the Boston Female Anti-Slavery Society, dragged through the streets of Boston with a rope around his body, and locked up in jail by the Mayor of that sedate city to protect him from his assailants. On the 4th of July, 1834, a meeting of the American Anti-Slavery Society was broken up in New York, and the house of Lewis Tappan was sacked by mob violence. A month later, in the city of Philadelphia, a mob against anti-slavery and colored men raged for three days and nights. On the 28th of July, 1836, a committee of thirteen citizens of Cincinnati, appointed by a public meeting, of whom Jacob Burnet, late United States Senator and Judge of the Supreme Court of Ohio, was chairman, waited upon Mr. James G. Birney and other members of the executive committee of the Ohio Anti-Slavery Society, under whose direction the "Philanthropist," an anti-slavery newspaper, was printed here, and informed them that unless they desisted from its publication the meeting would not be responsible for the consequences. Judge Burnet stated that the mob would consist of five thousand persons, and that two-thirds of the property holders of the city would join it. The committee gave Mr. Birney and his friends till the next day to consider the question, when they decided to make no terms with the rioters, and to abide the consequences. That night the office was sacked, and the press of the "Philanthropist" was thrown into the Ohio river.

But here was an oration delivered in the city of Baltimore in the year 1791, advancing the most extreme opinions, and it created not a ripple on the surface of Southern society.

That the opinions of the oration did not offend those to whom it was addressed, the official action of the Society, which is printed on the third page, attests. It is as follows:

"At a special meeting of the 'Maryland Society for Promoting the Abolition of Slavery and the Relief of Free Negroes and others Unlawfully held in Bondage,' held at Baltimore, July 4, 1791, unanimously

"*Resolved*, That the president present the thanks of the Society to Dr. George Buchanan, for the excellent oration by him delivered this day, and, at the same time, request a copy thereof in the name and for the use of the Society.

"Signed—Samuel Sterett, President; Alex. McKim, Vice-President; Joseph Townsend, Secretary."

The oration has this dedication:

"To the Honorable Thomas Jefferson, Esq., Secretary of State, whose partiotism since the American Revolution has been uniformly marked by a sincere, steady, and active attachment to the interest of his country, and whose literary abilities have distinguished him amongst the first of statesmen and philosophers—this oration is respectfully inscribed, as an humble testimony of the highest regard and esteem, by the Author."

The author was evidently a straight Democrat.

Seven years ago I copied this oration with the intention of reprinting it, with a brief historical introduction, supposing I could readily find the few facts I needed. But in this I was disappointed. Who was Dr. George Buchanan? That he was a member of the American Philosophical Society at Philadelphia was apparent on the title page; but that was all I could learn of him from books or inquiry. I then wrote to a historical friend in Baltimore to make inquiry for me there, and I received letters from the author's son, McKean Buchanan, senior paymaster in the United States navy, since deceased, and from two grandsons, Mr. George B.

Coale and Dr. Wm. Edw. Coale, giving full particulars, which I will condense:

Dr. George Buchanan was born on an estate, five miles from Baltimore, September 19, 1763, and for many years was a practicing physician in Baltimore. He was a son of Andrew Buchanan, who was also born in Maryland, and was General in the Continental troops of Maryland during the Revolution, and was one of the Commissioners who located the city of Baltimore. Dr. George Buchanan studied medicine and took a degree at Philadelphia. He then went to Europe and studied medicine at Edinburgh, and later at Paris, taking degrees at both places. Returning to Baltimore, he married Letitia, daughter of the Hon. Thomas McKean, an eminent jurist, who was a member of the Continental Congress, one of the Signers of the Declaration of Independence, and was Governor of Pennsylvania from 1799 to 1806. In 1806, Dr. Buchanan removed to Philadelphia, and died the next year of yellow fever, in the discharge of his official duties as Lazaretto physician. His eldest son was Paymaster McKean Buchanan, before mentioned. His youngest son was Franklin Buchanan, captain in the United States navy till he resigned, April 19, 1861, and went into the so-called Confederate navy. He was, with the rank of Admiral, in command of the iron-clad "Merrimac," and was wounded in the conflict of that vessel with the monitor "Ericsson," at Hampton Roads, March 9,

1862, and was later captured by Admiral Farragut in Mobile harbor.

"My brother," writes one of the grandsons, "told me that the last time he saw Henry Clay, Mr. Clay took his hand in both of his, and said, with great emphasis: 'It is to your grandfather that I owe my present position with regard to slavery. It was he who first pointed out to me the curse it entailed on the white man, and the manifold evils it brings with it.'"

In determining how far the sentiments contained in this oration were the current opinions of the time, it became necessary for me to know something definite of the "Maryland Society for the Abolition of Slavery," of the Virginia, the Pennsylvania, and other societies, which existed at that time. This information I could not obtain from anti-slavery books, or from the most prominent abolitionists whom I consulted. The matter seemed to have been forgotten, and it was the common idea that there was nothing worth remembering of the anti-slavery movement before 1830, when Mr. Garrison and his radical friends came upon the stage in Boston. For the want of the facts I needed, I laid aside the idea of reproducing the tract. The subject was brought again to mind by hearing the excellent paper, by Mr. S. E. Wright, our secretary, on the anti-slavery labors of Benjamin Lundy, which he read to this Club, a few months ago. The labors of Mr. Lundy began in 1816, and ended with his death in 1839. Quite recently I have obtained much of the information I needed.

Among the unknown facts to which I could get no clue at the time I have mentioned, were the names of the "Virginia Calculator" and the "Physician of New Orleans," whom Dr. Buchanan mentions with Phillis Wheatley, Ignatius Sancho, and Banneker, the Maryland astronomer, as being negroes who were distinguished for their literary and mathematical acquirements. Mr. Phillips had never heard of them, and he took the trouble to make inquiries among his anti-slavery friends, but without success.

A year or more after I had abandoned my little project, in looking over the files of the Columbian Centinal, printed in Boston, for 1790, I found under the date of December 29th, in the column of deaths, the following:

"DIED—Negro Tom, the famous African calculator, aged 80 years. He was the property of Mrs. Elizabeth Cox, of Alexandria. Tom was a very black man. He was brought to this country at the age of fourteen, and was sold as a slave with many of his unfortunate countrymen. This man was a prodigy. Though he could neither read nor write, he had perfectly acquired the use of enumeration. He could give the number of months, days, weeks, hours, minutes, and seconds, for any period of time that a person chose to mention, allowing in his calculations for all the leap years that happened in the time. He would give the number of poles, yards, feet, inches, and barley-corns in a given distance—say, the diameter of the earth's orbit—and in every calculation he would produce the true answer in less time than ninety-nine out of a hundred men would take with their pens. And what was, perhaps, more extraordinary, though interrupted in the progress of his calculations, and engaged in discourse upon any other subject, his operations were not thereby in the least deranged; he would go on where he left off, and could give any and all of the stages through which the calculation had passed.

"Thus died Negro Tom, this untaught arithmetician, this untutored scholar. Had his opportunities of improvement been equal to those of thousands of his fellow-men, neither the Royal Society of London, the Academy of Science at Paris, nor even a Newton himself need have been ashamed to acknowledge him a brother in science."

This obituary was doubtless extracted from a Southern newspaper. A fact once found is easily found again. I have come across the name of this unlettered negro prodigy many times since, with the substance of the facts already stated. In a letter which Dr. Benj. Rush, of Philadelphia, addressed to a gentleman in Manchester, England, he says that, hearing of the astonishing powers of Negro Tom, he, in company with other gentlemen passing through Virginia, sent for him. A gentleman of the company asked Tom how many seconds a man of seventy years, some odd months, weeks, and days had lived. He told the exact number in a minute and a half. The gentleman took a pen, and having made the calculation by figures, told the negro that he must be mistaken, as the number was too great. "'Top, massa," said the negro, "you hab left out de leap years." On including the leap years in the calculation, the number given by the negro was found to be correct.*

That Dr. Buchanan did not mention his name is explained by the fact that he died only six months before; and the audience, who had doubtless read the obituary notice just recited, or a similar one, knew who was meant. Besides, he was a native African, and had no name worth having. He was only Negro Tom. In Bishop Grégoire's work, however, he is ennobled by the name of Thomas Fuller, and in Mr. Needles' Memoir by the name of Thomas Tuller.†

---

*These facts may also be found in Steadman's Narrative of an Expedition to Surinam, vol. 2. p. 160; in Bishop Grégoire's "Enquiry into the Intellectual and Moral Faculties and Literature of Negroes," p. 153; in Edw. Needles' "Historical Memoir of the Pennsylvania Society for Promoting the Abolition of Slavery," p. 32; and in Brissot de Warville's New Travels in the United States, p. 287, ed. 1792.

†Mr. Needles says: "He was visited by William Hartshorn and Samuel Coates of this city (Philadelphia), and gave correct answers to all their questions—such as, how many seconds there are in a year and

Why Dr. Buchanan should have omitted to mention the name of "the New Orleans physician" does not appear, unless it be that he was equally well known. His name, I have found recently, was James Derham. Dr. Rush, in the American Museum for January, 1789, gave an account of Dr. Derham, who was then a practitioner of medicine at New Orleans, and, at the time the notice was written, was visiting in Philadelphia. He was twenty-six years of age, married, member of the Episcopal Church, and having a professional income of three thousand dollars a year. He was born in Philadelphia a slave, and was taught to read and write, and occasionally to compound medicines for his master, who was a physician. On the death of his master he was sold to the surgeon of the Sixteenth British regiment, and at the close of the war was sold to Dr. Robert Dove, of New Orleans, who employed him as an assistant in his business. He manifested such capacity, and so won the confidence and friendship of his master, that he was liberated on easy terms after two or three years' service, and entered into practice for himself. "I have conversed with him," says Dr. Rush, "upon most of the acute and epidemic diseases of the country where he lives. I expected to have suggested some new medi-

---

a half. In two minutes he answered 47,304,000. How many seconds in seventy years, seventeen days, twelve hours. In one minute and a half, 2,110,500,800. He multiplied nine figures by nine," etc., etc.

cines to him, but he suggested many more to me. He is very modest and engaging in his manners. He speaks French fluently, and has some knowledge of the Spanish."*

It was unfortunate that these incidents had not occurred early enough to have come to the knowledge of Mr. Jefferson before he wrote his "Notes on Virginia." These were precisely the kind of facts he was in quest of. He probably would have used them, and have strengthened the opinions he there expressed as to the intellectual capacity of the negro race.

His "Notes on Virginia" were written in 1781-2. His condemnation of slavery in that work is most emphatic. "The whole commerce between master and slave," he says, "is a perpetual exercise of the most boisterous passions; the most unremitting despotism on the one part, and degrading submission on the other. Our children see this and learn to imitate it. . . . The parent storms, the child looks on, catches the lineaments of wrath, puts on the same airs in the circle of smaller slaves, gives loose to his worst of passions; and thus nursed, educated, and daily exercised in tyranny, can not but be stamped by it with odious peculiarities. The man must be a prodigy who can retain his manners and morals undepraved by such circumstances. With

---

*Accounts of these two black men were prepared by Dr. Rush, for the information of the London Society.

what execration should the statesman be loaded, who, permitting one-half the citizens thus to trample on the rights of the other, transforms those into despots and these into enemies—destroys the morals of the one part, and the *amor patriæ* of the other? . . Can the liberties of a nation be thought secure when we have removed their only firm basis—a conviction in the minds of men that these liberties are the gift of God; that they are not to be violated but with His wrath? Indeed, I tremble for my country, when I reflect that God is just—that His justice can not sleep forever." Pp. 270--272, ed. Lond., 1787.

On the practical question, "What shall be done about it?" Mr Jefferson's mind wavered; he was in doubt. How can slavery be abolished? He proposed, in Virginia, a law, which was rejected, making all free who were born after the passage of the act. And here again he hesitated. What will become of these people after they are free? What are their capacities? He had never seen an educated negro. He had heard of Phillis Wheatley and Ignatius Sancho. He did not highly estimate the poetry of the one, or the sentimental letters of the other. He was willing to admit, however, that a negro could write poetry and sentimental letters. Beyond this all was in doubt. He regarded it as highly probable that they could do nothing more. He says: "Comparing them by their faculties of memory, reason, and imagination, it appears to me that in memory they are equal to the whites; in reason much inferior, as I think one could scarcely be found capable of tracing and comprehending the investigations of Euclid"—p. 232. He doubtingly adds: "The opinion that they are inferior in the faculties of reason and imagination must be hazarded with great diffidence. To justify a general conclusion requires many observations"—p. 238. The opportunity for making these observations he had never had.

It so happened that soon after writing this, Banneker, the Maryland negro astronomer, who had distinguished himself in the very faculty of mathematical reasoning which Mr. Jefferson had supposed no negro possessed, sent him his Almanac, with a letter. To the letter Mr. Jefferson replied as follows:

"I thank you sincerely for your letter of the 19th instant, and for the Almanac it contained. Nobody wishes more than I do to see such proofs as you exhibit, that nature has given to our black brethren talents equal to those of other colors of men, and that the appearance of a want of them is owing merely to the degraded condition of their existence, both in Africa and America. I can add with truth, that nobody wishes more ardently to see a good system commenced for raising the condition, both of their body and mind, to what it ought to be, as fast as the imbecility of their present existence, and other circumstances which can not be neglected, will admit. I have taken the liberty of sending your Almanac to Monsieur de Condorcet, Secretary of the Academy of Sciences at Paris, and member of the Philanthropic Society, because I consider it a document to which your color had a right for their justification against the doubts which have been entertained of them. I am, with great esteem, sir, your most obedient, humble servant,

"THOS. JEFFERSON."*

The next instances of precocious black men which must have come to his knowledge were, doubtless, Negro Tom, in whom the mathematical faculty was strangely developed, and James Derham, the New Orleans physician. If Mr. Jefferson had rewritten his "Notes," he would, probably, have included mathematics and medicine among the special subjects which were peculiarly adapted to the capacities of the negro mind.

It was not the question of the natural rights of the negro, the prejudice of color, nor of the ruinous improvidence of the system of slavery, that controlled the decision in Mr. Jefferson's mind, as to the methods by which the system should be terminated. On these points, he was as radical as the extremest abolitionist; but he could not satisfy himself as to the mental capacity of the negro—whether he had the full complement of human capabilities, and the qualifications for equality

---

* Works, iii, p. 291.

of citizenship with the white man; for he saw that emancipation, without expatriation, meant nothing else than giving the black man all the rights of citizenship. The theory that the negro is a decaudalized ape, a progressing chimpanzee, is an invention of the last forty years, and contemporaneous with the discovery that the Bible sanctions slavery. He was, on the whole, inclined to the opinion that they were an inferior race of beings, and that their residence, in a state of freedom, among white men was incompatible with the happiness of both. He thought they had better be emancipated, and sent out of the country. He therefore took up with the colonization scheme long before the Colonization Society was founded. He did not feel sure on this point. With his practical mind, he could not see how a half million of slaves could be sent out of the country, even if they were voluntarily liberated;* where they

---

* In a letter to M. de Meusnier, dated January 24, 1786, Mr. Jefferson says: " I conjecture there are six hundred and fifty thousand negroes in the five southermost states, and not fifty thousand in the rest. In most of the latter, effectual measures have been taken for their future emancipation. In the former nothing is done toward that. The disposition to emancipate them is strongest in Virginia. Those who desire it, form, as yet, the minority of the whole state, but it bears a respectable proportion to the whole, in numbers and weight of character; and it is constantly recruiting by the addition of nearly the whole of the young men as fast as they come into public life. I flatter myself that it will take place there at some period of time not very distant. In Maryland and North Carolina, a very few are disposed to emanci-

should be sent to, or how unwilling masters could be compelled to liberate their slaves. While, therefore, he did not favor immediate emancipation, he was zealous for no other scheme.

Bishop Grégoire, of Paris, felt deeply hurt at Mr. Jefferson's low estimate of the negro's mental capacity, and wrote to him a sharp letter on the subject. Later, the Bishop sent a copy of his own book on the Literature of Negroes.* Acknowledging the receipt of the Bishop's book, Mr. Jefferson says:

"Be assured that no person living wishes more sincerely than I do, to see a complete refutation of the doubts I have myself entertained and expressed on the grade and understanding allotted to them by nature, and to find that, in this respect, they are on a par with ourselves. My doubts were the result of personal observation on the limited sphere of my own State, where the opportunities for the development of their genius were not favorable, and those of exercising it still less

---

pate. In South Carolina and Georgia, not the smallest symptom of it; but, on the contrary, these two states and North Carolina continue importations of slaves. These have long been prohibited in all the other states." Works, ix, p. 290.

* "De la Littérature des Nègres; ou Recherches sur leurs Facultès Intellectuelles, leurs Qualités Morales et leur Litterature, Paris, 1808." 8vo. The work was translated by D. B. Warden, Secretary of the American Legation at Paris, and printed at Brooklyn, New York, in 1810.

so. I expressed them, therefore, with great hesitation; but whatever be their degree of talent, it is no measure of their rights. Because Sir Isaac Newton was superior to others in understanding, he was not therefore lord of the person and property of others. On this subject they are gaining daily in the opinions of nations, and hopeful advances are making toward their re-establishment on an equal footing with other colors of the human family. I pray you, therefore, to accept my thanks for the many instances you have enabled me to observe of respectable intelligence in that race of men, which can not fail to have effect in hastening the day of their relief." Works, v, p. 429.

Writing to another person a few months later, he alludes to this letter and says: "As to Bishop Grégoire, I wrote him a very soft answer. It was impossible for a doubt to be more tenderly or hesitatingly expressed than it was in the Notes on Virginia; and nothing was, or is, further from my intentions than to enlist myself as a champion of a fixed opinion, where I have only expressed a doubt." Works, v, p. 476.

Mr. Jefferson never got beyond his doubt; and Bishop Grégoire resented his passive position by omitting Mr. Jefferson's name from a list of fourteen Americans, which included Mr. Madison, William Pinkney, Dr. Benj. Rush, Timothy Dwight, Col. Humphreys, and Joel Barlow, to whom, with other philanthropists, he dedicated his book.

Washington, Madison, Patrick Henry, George Mason, and nearly all the public men of Virginia and Maryland of that period were in much the same state of mind as Jefferson.* So was Henry Clay at a later period.

Mr. Jefferson, in August, 1785, wrote a letter to Dr. Richard Price, of London, author of a treatise on Liberty, in which very advanced opinions were taken on

---

*Gen. Washington, although a slaveholder, put on record throughout his voluminous correspondence his detestation of the system of slavery, as practiced at the South.

M. Brissot de Warville, in connection with Gen. Lafayette and other French philanthropists, early in the year 1788, formed at Paris the Philanthropic Society of the Friends of Negroes, to co-operate with those in America and London, in procuring the abolition of the traffic in, and the slavery of, the blacks. In furtherance of this object, M. Brissot de Warville delivered an oration in Paris, February 17, 1788, which was translated and printed by the Pennsylvania Abolition Society, in Philadelphia, the next year. In May of the same year, he arrived in the United States, and wrote the most impartial and instructive book of travels in America (with the exception of M. de Tocqueville's), that has ever been made by a foreigner, of which several editions in English were printed in London. His principles brought him into intimate relations with persons who held anti-slavery sentiments, and his work gives a very interesting epitome of the prevalence of those sentiments at that period.

He visited General Washington at Mount Vernon, and conversed with him freely on the subject of slavery. He states that the General had three hundred slaves distributed in log houses in different parts of his plantation of ten thousand acres. "They were treated," he said,

the slavery question. Concerning the prevalence of anti-slavery opinions at that period, he says: "Southward of the Chesapeake your book will find but few readers concurring with it in sentiment on the subject of slavery. From the mouth to the head of the Chesapeake, the bulk of the people will approve its theory, and it will find a respectable minority, a minority ready to adopt it in practice; which, for weight and worth of character, preponderates against the greater num-

---

" with the greatest humanity; well fed, well clothed, and kept to moderate labor. They bless God without ceasing for having given them so good a master. It is a task worthy of a soul so elevated, so pure and so disinterested, to begin the revolution in Virginia to prepare the way for the emancipation of the negroes. This great man declared to me that he rejoiced at what was doing in other States on the subject [of emancipation—alluding to the recent formation of several state societies]; that he sincerely desired the extension of it in his own State; but he did not dissemble that there were still many obstacles to be overcome; that it was dangerous to strike too vigorously at a prejudice which had begun to diminish; that time, patience, and information would not fail to vanquish it. Almost all the Virginians, he added, believe that the liberty of the blacks can not soon become general. This is the reason why they do not wish to form a society which may give dangerous ideas to their slaves. There is another obstacle—the great plantations of which the state is composed, render it necessary for men to live so dispersed that frequent meetings of a society would be difficult.

"I replied, that the Virginians were in an error; that evidently, sooner or later, the negroes would obtain their liberty everywhere. It is then for the interest of your countrymen to prepare the way to such a revolution, by endeavoring to reconcile the restitution of

ber who have not the courage to divest their families of a property which, however, keeps their consciences unquiet. Northward of the Chesapeake you may find, here and there, an opponent to your doctrine, as you find, here and there, a robber and murderer, but in no greater number. In that part of America there are but few slaves, and they can easily disincumber themselves of them; and emancipation is put in such a train

the rights of the blacks, with the interest of the whites. The means necessary to be taken to this effect can only be the work of a society; and it is worthy the saviour of America to put himself at the head, and to open the door of liberty to 300,000 unhappy beings of his own State. He told me that he desired the formation of a society, and that he would second it; but that he did not think the moment favorable. Doubtless more elevated views filled his soul. The destiny of America was just ready to be placed a second time in his hands." Ed. of 1792, pp. 290, 291.

"The strongest objection to freeing the negroes lies in the character, the manners, and habits of the Virginians. They seem to enjoy the sweat of slaves. They are fond of hunting; they love the display of luxury, and disdain the idea of labor. This order of things will change when slavery shall be no more." Id., p. 281.

Patrick Henry, in the Virginia Constitutional Convention, opposing the adoption of the Federal Constitution, said: "In this State there are 236,000 blacks. May Congress not say that every black man must fight? Did we not see a little of this in the last war? We were not so hard pushed as to make emancipation general; but acts of Assembly passed that every slave who would go to the army should be free. Another thing will contribute to bring this event [emancipation] about. Slavery is detested. We feel its fatal effects; we deplore it with all

that in a few years there will be no slaves northward of Maryland. In Maryland I do not find such a disposition to begin the redress of this enormity as in Virginia. These [the inhabitants of Virginia] have sucked in the principles of liberty, as it were, with their mothers' milk, and it is to these I look with anxiety to turn the fate of this question. Be not, therefore, discouraged. The College of William and Mary in Williamsburg,

---

the pity of humanity. Have they [Congress] not power to provide for the general defense and welfare? May they not think that these call for the abolition of slavery? May they not pronounce all slaves free, and will they not be warranted by that power?

"I repeat it again, that it would rejoice my very soul, that every one of my fellow-beings were emancipated. As we ought, with gratitude, to admire that decree of Heaven which has numbered us among the free, we ought to lament and deplore the necessity of holding our fellow-men in bondage. But is it practicable, by any human means, to liberate them without producing the most dreadful and ruinous consequences?" Elliott's Debates, Va., pp. 590, 591.

George Mason, in the same convention, speaking against article 1, section 9, of the Constitution, which forbids Congress from prohibiting the importation of slaves before the year 1808, said: "It [the importation of slaves] was one of the great causes of our separation from Great Britain. Its exclusion has been a principal object of this State, and most of the States of the Union. The augmentation of slaves weakens the States; and such a trade is diabolical in itself, and disgraceful to mankind: yet, by this Constitution, it is continued for twenty years. As much as I value a union of all the States, I would not admit the Southern States into the Union, unless they agree to the discontinuance of this disgraceful trade, because it brings weakness, and not strength, to the Union." Elliott's Debates, Va., p. 452.

since the remodeling of its plan, is the place where are collected together all the young men of Virginia under preparation for public life. There they are under the direction (most of them) of a Mr. George Wythe [Professor of Law from 1779 to 1789], one of the most virtuous of characters, and whose sentiments on the subject of slavery are unequivocal. I am satisfied if you could resolve to address an exhortation to these young men, with all the eloquence of which you are master, that its influence on the future decision of this important question would be great, perhaps decisive." * Works, i, p. 377.

---

*Mr. Jefferson's doubts, and his timidity, as a person of political aspirations, in treating the subject of slavery in a practical manner, reduced his conduct to the verge of cowardice, if not of duplicity. While writing to Dr. Price in this assured tone, and urging him to exhort the young men of the College of William and Mary, on the evils of slavery, he was afraid to have these same students see what he had himself written on the same subject, in his "Notes on Virginia." M. de Chastelleux had written to him desiring to print some extracts from the "Notes on Virginia," in the *Journal de Physique*. Mr. Jefferson replied, June 7, 1785, only two months before he wrote the above letter to Dr. Price, saying: "I am not afraid that you should make any extracts you please for the *Journal de Physique*, which come within their plan of publication. The strictures on slavery, and on the constitution of Virginia, are not of that kind, and they are the parts which I do not wish to have made public; at least, till I know whether their publication would do most harm or good. It is possible that, in my own country, these strictures might produce an irritation which would indispose the people toward the two great objects I have in view; that

There was great progress in anti-slavery sentiment between 1785 and 1791, when Maryland was fully awake, as we see from Dr. Buchanan's Oration. In proof of this progress, it may be stated that, in 1784, Mr. Jefferson drew up an ordinance for the government of the Western territories, in which he inserted an article prohibiting slavery in the territories after the year 1800. On reporting the ordinance to the Continental Congress, the article prohibiting slavery was forthwith stricken out, and the report, as amended, was accepted; but the ordinance itself was a dead letter. Three years later, the celebrated Ordinance of 1787, for the organ-

---

is, the emancipation of their slaves, and the settlement of their constitution on a firmer and more permanent basis. If I learn from thence that they will not produce that effect, I have printed and reserved just copies enough to be able to give one to every young man at the College." Works, i, p. 339.

Writing from Paris, August 13, 1786, to George Wythe, Mr. Jefferson says: "Madison, no doubt, informed you why I sent only a single copy of my 'Notes' to Virginia. Being assured by him that they will not do the harm I had apprehended; but, on the contrary, may do some good, I propose to send thither the copies remaining on hand, which are fewer than I intended." Works, ii, p. 6. Mr. Madison's communications to Mr. Jefferson on the subject are in his "Letters and other Writings," i, pp. 202, 211. M. Brissot de Warville proposed to Mr. Jefferson to become a member of the Philanthropic Society of Paris. Mr. Jefferson replied, February 12, 1788, as follows: "I am very sensible of the honor you propose to me, of becoming a member of the society for the abolition of the slave trade. You know that nobody wishes more ardently to see an abolition, not

ization of the Northwest Territory, embracing what is now the States of Ohio, Indiana, Illinois, Michigan, and Wisconsin, was reported by a committee consisting of Edward Carrington of Virginia, Nathan Dane of Massachusetts, Richard Henry Lee of Virginia, John Kean of South Carolina, and Melancthon Smith of New York, acting under the advice of Dr. Mannasseh Cutler, citizen of Massachusetts, who was then in New York, attending the sessions of Congress, for the purpose of buying land for the Ohio Company, which made, the next year, the first English settlement in that Territory, at Marietta. The Ordinance provided that "there shall be neither slavery nor involuntary servitude in the

---

only of the trade, but of the condition of slavery; and certainly nobody will be more willing to encounter every sacrifice for that object. But the influence and information of the friends to this proposition in France, will be far above the need of my association. I am here as a public servant; and those whom I serve, having never yet been able to give their voice against the practice, it is decent for me to avoid too public demonstration of my wishes to see it abolished. Without serving the cause here, it might render me less able to serve it beyond the water. I trust you will be sensible of the prudence of those motives, therefore, which govern my conduct on this occasion, and be assured of my wishes for the success of your undertaking." Works, ii, p. 357.

Compare this record with Mr. Garrison's, which he put forth in the "Liberator," in 1831. He had been accused of using plain and harsh language. He says: "My country is the world, and my countrymen are all mankind. I will be as harsh as truth, and as uncompromising as justice. I am in earnest; I will not equivocate; I will not excuse; I will not retreat a single inch; and *I will be heard.*"

said Territory." It was passed without debate, or the offer (except by the committee) of an amendment, by the vote of every state. A few years earlier or later, such a vote would have been impossible.* Just before this date, commenced the great Southern awakening on the subject of slavery, of which so little is now known, and of which Dr. Buchanan's Oration is an illustration.

There never has been a time since 1619, when the first slave ship, a Dutch man-of-war, entered James river, in Virginia, when in our country there were not persons protesting against the wickedness and impolicy of the African slave trade and of the domestic slave system. Slavery was introduced into the American colonies, against the wishes of the settlers, by the avarice of British traders and with the connivance of the British government. Just previous to the Revolution, the

---

*Mr. Jeffersons' indecision in dealing with an institution he so much abhorred, is seen in the anti-slavery provision of his ordinance. He would allow slavery to get a foot-hold in the western territories, and at the end of sixteen years would prohibit it. By southern votes, this clause was fortunately stricken out. Every northern state voted to retain Mr. Jefferson's fifth article of compact, and its rejection, which was regarded at the time, as a public calamity, was soon seen to be a piece of good fortune. Timothy Pickering, writing to Rufus King, nearly a year later (March 8, 1785), says: "I should indeed have objected to the period proposed (1800) for the exclusion of slavery; for the admission of it for a day, or an hour, ought to have been forbidden. It will be infinitely easier to prevent the evil at first, than to eradicate it, or check it, at any future time. To suffer the continuance of slaves

Colony of Massachusetts made several attempts to relieve itself of the incubus, and the acts of the General Court were smothered or vetoed by three successive Governors, under the plea that they had such instructions from England. In 1772, the Assembly of Virginia petitioned the throne of England to stop the importation of slaves, using language as follows: "We are encouraged to look up to the throne and implore your Majesty's paternal assistance in averting a calamity of a most alarming nature. The importation of slaves into the colonies from the coast of Africa hath long been considered as a trade of great inhumanity, and under its present encouragement, we have much reason to fear will endanger the very existence of your Majesty's dominions. Deeply impressed with these sentiments, we most humbly beseech your Majesty to remove all restraints on your Majesty's Governors of this colony,

till they can be gradually emancipated, in states already overrun with them, may be pardonable; but to introduce them into a territory where none now exist, can never be forgiven. For God's sake, let one more effort be made to prevent so terrible a calamity."

Mr. King, eight days later, moved, in Congress, to attach an article of compact to Mr. Jefferson's ordinance, in the place of the one stricken out, in substantially the words that stand in the Ordinance of 1787: "That there shall be neither slavery nor involuntary servitude in any of the States described in the resolve of Congress of April 23, 1784." The matter was referred to a committee; but was never taken up and acted on. If Mr. King's resolution had passed, it would have excluded slavery from Kentucky, Tennessee, and all the Western territories.

which inhibit to their assisting to such laws as might check so very pernicious a commerce." No notice was taken of the petition by the crown. This was the principal grievance complained of by Virginia at the commencement of the revolutionary war.

The limits allowed me forbid my giving even a sketch of legislative action, of the opinions of great men, of the labors of Samuel Sewall, George Keith, Samuel Hopkins, William Burling, Ralph Sandiford, Anthony Benezet, Benjamin Lay, John Woolman, and others, and of the literature of the subject, from the beginning of the irrepressible conflict in 1619 down to the period we are considering.*

---

*George Keith, a Quaker, about the year 1693, printed a pamphlet in which he charged his own religious denomination, "that they should set their negroes at liberty, after some reasonable time of service." Samuel Sewall, Judge of the Superior Court of Massachusetts, in 1700, printed a tract against slavery, entitled, "The Selling of Joseph, a Memorial," which he gave to each member of the General Court, to clergymen, and to literary gentlemen with whom he was acquainted. This tract is reprinted in Moore's "Notes on Slavery in Massachusetts," p. 83. These were the earliest publications on slavery in this country. Dr. Franklin having mentioned Keith's pamphlet, says: "About the year 1728 or 1729, I myself printed a book for Ralph Sandyford, another of your friends in this city, against keeping negroes in slavery; two editions of which he distributed gratis. And about the year 1736, I printed another book on the same subject for Benjamin Lay, who also professed being one of your friends, and he distributed the books chiefly among them." Works, x, 403.

The earliest statute for the suppression of slavery in the colonies

The revolutionary war, and the questions which then arose, turned the thoughts of men, as never before, to the injustice and impolicy of slavery. At the first general Congress of the colonies, held at Philadelphia in 1774, Mr. Jefferson presented an exposition of rights, in which he says: "The abolition of slavery is the greatest object of desire in these colonies, when it was unhappily introduced in their infant state." Among the "articles of association" adopted by that Congress, October 20, 1774, was this: "That we will neither import, nor purchase any slave imported, after the first day of December next, nor will we hire our vessels, nor sell our commodities or manufactures to those who are concerned in the slave trade."

The first anti-slavery society, in this or any other

may be seen in Rhode Island Records, i, 248, under the date of May 19, 1652, which, however, was never enforced.

The earliest legislative protest against man-stealing, is the following: "The General Court, conceiving themselves bound by the first opportunity, to bear witness against the heinous and crying sin of man-stealing, and also to prescribe such timely redress for what is past, and such a law for the future, as may sufficiently deter all others belonging to us to have to do in such vile and most odious courses, justly abhorred of all good and just men—do order that the negro interpreter, with others unlawfully taken, be, by the first opportunity, (at the charge of the country for present) sent to his native country of Guinea, and a letter with him of the indignation of the Court thereabouts, and justice hereof—desiring our honored Governor would please to put this order in execution." November 4, 1646, Massachusetts Records, ii, p. 168.

country, was formed April 14, 1775, at the Sun Tavern, on Second street, in Philadelphia. The original members of this society were mostly, and perhaps all of them, Friends or Quakers. This religious society had, for many years, earnestly protested against slavery. As early as 1696 the yearly meeting had cautioned its members against encouraging the bringing in of any more negroes. In 1743, and, again in 1755, the annual query was made, whether their members were clear of importing or buying slaves. In 1758, those who disobeyed the advice of the yearly meeting were placed under discipline; and in 1776, those who continued to hold slaves over the lawful age, were disowned.*

The first anti-slavery society took the name of "The Society for the Relief of Free Negroes unlawfully held in Bondage."† The society met four times in 1775, and on

---

*Patrick Henry, in a letter dated January 18; 1773, to Robert Pleasants, afterwards President of the Virginia Abolition Society, said: "Believe me, I shall honor the Quakers for their noble efforts to abolish slavery. It is a debt we owe to the purity of our religion to show that it is at variance with that law that warrants slavery. I exhort you to persevere in so worthy a resolution. I believe a time will come when an opportunity will be offered to abolish this lamentable evil." Wm. Goodell's Slavery and Anti-Slavery, p. 70.

†The preamble of the Constitution then adopted was as follows: "Whereas, there are in this and the neighboring states a number of negroes and others kept in a state of slavery, who, we apprehend, from different causes and circumstances, are justly entitled to their freedom by the laws and Constitution under which we live, could their particular

account of the war no meeting occurred again till February, 1784. I was so fortunate to find among some pamphlets, presented to our Public Library a short time since, an original copy of the "Rules and Regulations" of this society, printed in 1784, which I have here.* Regu-

---

cases be candidly and openly debated, and evidence to the best advantage for them procured; but as in their situation, they, being tied by the strong cords of oppression, are rendered incapable of asserting their freedom, and many through this inability remain unjustly in bondage through life; it therefore has appeared necessary that some aid should be extended towards such poor unhappy sufferers, wherever they may be discovered, either in this city or its neighborhood; and, as loosing the bonds of wickedness, and setting the oppressed free, is evidently a duty incumbent on all professors of Christianity, but more especially at a time when justice, liberty, and the laws of the land are the general topics among most ranks and stations of men. Therefore, being desirous, as much as in us lies, to contribute towards obtaining relief for all such as are kept thus unjustly in thralldom, we have agreed to inspect and take charge of all the particular cases which may hereafter come to our knowledge; and that our good intentions may operate the more successfully, and be of general utility to such as stand in need of our assistance, we judge it expedient to form ourselves into a regular society, by the name of "The Society for the Relief of Free Negroes unlawfully held in Bondage." The officers elected were John Baldwin, President; Samuel Davis, Treasurer; Thomas Harrison, Secretary. Six members were also appointed a Committee of Inspection, and a number of cases were forthwith committed to their care. Edw. Needles's Historical Memoir of the Pennsylvania Society, p. 15.

*Appended to the Rules and Regulations, is the act of 1780, providing for the gradual abolition of slavery in Pennsylvania. The members of the Philadelphia Society were especially active in procuring

lar meetings were held till April, 1787, when the constitution was revised and made to include the "Abolition of Slavery" as well as the "Relief of Free Negroes" and Dr. Benjamin Franklin was chosen president, and Benjamin Rush, secretary, both signers of the Declaration of Independence.*

---

the passage of this act. Anthony Benezet held private interviews with every member of the government on the subject. The act passed the assembly by a vote of 34 to 21. The minority entered a protest against it on several grounds: First, because it would be offensive to other states, and would weaken the bonds of union with them; Second, while they approved of the justice and humanity of manumitting slaves in time of peace, this was not the proper time; Third, they did not approve of slaves becoming citizens, of their voting and being voted for, of intermarrying with white persons, etc.; Fourth, because the motion to postpone to the next session of the Assembly had been overruled.

*James Pemberton and Jonathan Penrose were chosen Vice-Presidents; James Starr, Treasurer; and Wm. Lewis, John D. Cox, Miers Fisher, and Wm. Rawle, Counselors. Thirty-six new members were elected at this meeting. The preamble of the new organization was as follows: "It having pleased the Creator of the world to make of one flesh all the children of men, it becomes them to consult and promote each other's happiness, as members of the same family, however diversified they may be by color, situation, religion, or different states of society. It is more especially the duty of those persons who profess to maintain for themselves the rights of human nature, and who acknowledge the obligations of Christianity, to use such means as are in their power to extend the blessings of freedom to every part of the human race; and in a more particular manner to such of their fellow-creatures as are entitled to freedom by the laws and constitutions of

The society entered with zeal upon its mission, circulating its documents, and opening a correspondence with eminent men in the United States and in Europe.*

any of the United States, and who, notwithstanding, are detained in bondage by fraud or violence. From a full conviction of the truth and obligation of these principles; from a desire to diffuse them wherever the miseries and vices of slavery exist, and in humble confidence of the favor and support of the Father of mankind, the subscribers have associated themselves, under the title of 'The Pennsylvania Society for promoting the Abolition of Slavery, and the Relief of Free Negroes unlawfully held in Bondage, and for improving the condition of the African race.'" Needles's Memoir, p. 30.

*The secretaries were directed to have one thousand copies of the Constitution printed, together with the names of the officers of the society, and the acts of the Legislature of Pennsylvania for the gradual abolition of slavery. They were also to prepare letters to be sent to each of the Governors of the United States, with a copy of the Constitution and laws, and a copy of Clarkson's essay on "The Commerce and Slavery of the Africans." They were also directed to write letters to the Society in New York, to Thomas Clarkson and Dr. Price of London, and to the Abbé Raynall, in France. Needles's Memoir, p. 30.

Dr. Franklin drew up a "Plan for Improving the Condition of the Free Blacks." It embraced: First, a Committee of Inspection, who shall superintend the morals, general conduct, and ordinary situation of the free negroes, and afford them advice and instruction, protection from wrongs, and other friendly offices. Second, a Committee of Guardians, who shall place out children and young people with suitable persons, that they may, during a moderate time of apprenticeship or servitude, learn some trade, or other business of subsistence. Third, a Committee of Education, who shall superintend the school instruction,

The New York "Society for Promoting the Manumission of Slaves" was organized January 25, 1785, and John Jay was the first president. On being ap-

of the children and youth of the free blacks. Fourth, a Committee of Employ, who shall endeavor to procure constant employment for those free negroes who are able to work, as the want of this would occasion poverty, idleness, and many vicious habits. The entire plan may be seen in Dr. Franklin's Works, ii, pp. 513, 514. Immediately following, in the same volume, is "An Address to the Public," from the Pennsylvania Society, also written by Dr. Franklin, in aid of raising funds for carrying out the purposes of the society.

M. Brissot de Warville, who visited the New York and Philadelphia Societies in 1788, says: "It is certainly a misfortune that such societies do not exist in Virginia and Maryland, for it is to the persevering zeal of those of Philadelphia and New York, that we owe the progress of this [anti-slavery] revolution in America, and the formation of the Society in London." He speaks of the impressions he received in attending the meetings of these societies. "What serenity in the countenances of the members! What simplicity in their discourses; candor in their discussions; beneficence and energy in their decisions! With what joy they learned that a like Society was formed in Paris! They hastened to publish it in their gazettes, and likewise a translation of the first discourse [his own] pronounced in that society. These beneficent societies are at present contemplating new projects for the completion of their work of justice and humanity. They are endeavoring to form similar institutions in other states, and have succeeded in the state of Delaware. The business of these societies is not only to extend light and information to legislatures and to the people at large, and to form the blacks by early instruction in the duties of citizens; but they extend gratuitous protection to them in all cases of individual oppression, and make it their duty to watch over the execution of the laws, which

pointed Chief Justice of the United States, he resigned, and Alexander Hamilton was appointed to his place. This society circulated gratuitously Dr. Samuel Hopkins's Dialogue on Slavery, and Address to Slaveholders, and other documents. In 1787, the Society offered a

have been obtained in their favor. Mr. Myers Fisher, one of the first lawyers of Philadelphia, is always ready to lend them his assistance, which he generally does with success, and always without reward. These societies have committees in different parts of the country to take notice of any infractions of these laws of liberty, and to propose to the legislature such amendments as experience may require"—pp. 291–294.

In an appendix, written in 1791, he says: "My wishes have not been disappointed. The progress of these societies is rapid in the United States; there is one already formed even in Virginia." His English translator adds, that there has also one been formed in the state of Connecticut.

In Needles' Memoir are the names of the following persons who were officers, and served on committees, of the Pennsylvania Society before the year 1800: John Baldwin, Samuel Davis, Thomas Harrison, Anthony Benezet, Thomas Meredith, John Todd, James Starr, Samuel Richards, James Whiteall, Wm. Lippencott, John Thomas, Benjamin Horner, John Evans, Lambert Wilmore, Edward Brooks, Thomas Armit, John Warner, Daniel Sidrick, Thomas Barton, Robert Evans Benj. Miers, Robert Wood, John Eldridge, Jonathan Penrose, Wm., Lewis, Francis Baily, Norris Jones, Tench Cox, Wm. Jackson, Benj. Rush, Benj. Franklin, James Pemberton, John D. Cox, Wm. Rawle, Miers Fisher, Temple Franklin, John Andrews, Richard Peters, Thomas Paine, Caleb Lownes, S. P. Griffiths, John Olden, John Todd, Jr., John Kaighn, Wm. Rogers, Benj. Say, Thomas Parker, Robert Waln, Samuel Pancoast, Thomas Savery, Robert Taggert,

gold medal for the best discourse, at the public commencement of Columbia College, on the injustice and cruelty of the slave-trade, and the fatal effects of slavery. The London Society was organized July 17, 1787; the Paris Society in February, 1788;* and the Delaware Society the same year.† The Maryland

John Poultney, Wm. Zane, Joseph Moore, Joseph Budd, Wm. McIllhenny, Samuel Baker, Jonathan Willis, Richard Jones, Ellis Yarnall, Thomas Arnott, Philip Benezet, Samuel Emlen, Jr., Jacob Shoemaker, Jr., Richard Wells, Bart. Wistar, R. Wells, J. McCrea, Nathan Boys, J. Proctor, Robert Patterson, Walter Franklin, Edward Farris, John Ely, Samuel M. Fox, Sallows Shewell. John Woodside, Wm. Garrum, Thomas Ross, Joseph Sharpless, Joseph Cruikshanks, G. Williams, Wm. Webb, Geo. Williams, David Thomas, Samuel Bettle, Edward Garrigues.

*At the end of M. Brissot de Warville's oration at Paris, February 19, 1788, on the necessity of establishing such a society, is a note, which states that, after the Paris Society had been formed, "in the space of six weeks, ninety others, distinguished for their nobility, for their offices, and as men of letters, have made application to be admitted into the Society. The Marquis de la Fayette is one of the founders of this Society, and he gives it a support, so much the more laudable, as the Society of Paris has many great difficulties to encounter, which are unknown to the societies in London and America."

†M. Brissot, writing in September, 1788, speaks of the Delaware Society as then existing. Warner Mifflin was its most enterprising member. M. Brissot says of him : " One of the most ardent petitioners to Congress in this cause was the respectable Warner Mifflin. His zeal was rewarded with atrocious calumnies, which he always answered with mildness, forgiveness, and argument "—p. 300. A petition which

Society was formed September 8, 1789,* and the same year the Rhode Island Society was organized in the house of Dr. Hopkins, at Newport. In 1790, the Connecticut Society was formed, of which Dr. Ezra Stiles, President of Yale College, and Judge Simeon

---

Mr. Mifflin made to Congress in November, 1792, for the abolition of slavery, was, by vote of the House, returned to him by the clerk. Annals of Congress, iii, p. 71. On March 23, 1790, the following resolution on the subject of emancipation, after discussion in committee of the whole House, was adopted: " That Congress have no authority to interfere in the emancipation of slaves, or in the treatment of them in any of the States, it remaining with the several States alone to provide any regulations therein which humanity and true policy may require." Annals, i, p. 1523.

*Constitution of the Maryland Society for promoting the Abolition of Slavery, and the Relief of Free Negroes and others unlawfully held in Bondage.

The present attention of Europe and America to slavery, seems to constitute that crisis in the minds of men, when the united endeavors of a few may greatly influence the public opinion, and produce, from the transient sentiment of the times, effects, extensive, lasting, and useful.

The common Father of mankind created all men free and equal; and his great command is, that we love our neighbor as ourselves— doing unto all men as we would they should do unto us. The human race, however varied in color or intellects, are all justly entitled to liberty; and it is the duty and the interest of nations and individuals, enjoying every blessing of freedom, to remove this dishonor of the Christian character from amongst them. From the fullest impression of the truth of these principles; from an earnest wish to bear our testimony against slavery in all its forms, to spread it abroad as far as the

Baldwin, were the president and secretary. The Virginia Society was formed in 1791; and the New Jersey Society in 1792.

sphere of our influence may extend, and to afford our friendly assistance to those who may be engaged in the same undertaking; and in the humblest hope of support from that Being, who takes, as an offering to himself, what we do for each other—

We, the subscribers, have formed ourselves into the "MARYLAND SOCIETY for promoting the ABOLITION OF SLAVERY, and the RELIEF OF FREE NEGROES and OTHERS unlawfully held in bondage."

THE CONSTITUTION.

I. The officers of the Society are a president, vice-president, secretary, treasurer, four counselors, an electing-committee of twelve, an acting-committee of six members. All these, except the acting-committee, shall be chosen annually by ballot, on the first seventh-day, called Saturday, in the month called January.

II. The president, and in his absence the vice-president, shall subscribe all the public acts of the Society.

III. The president, and in his absence, the vice-president, shall moreover have the power of calling a special meeting of the Society whenever he shall judge proper, or six members require it.

IV. The secretary shall keep fair records of the proceedings of the Society; he shall also conduct the correspondence of the Society, with a committee of three appointed by the president; and all letters on the business of the Society are to be addressed to him.

V. Corresponding members shall be appointed by the electing-committee. Their duty shall be to communicate to the secretary and his assistants any information, that may promote the purposes of this institution, which shall be transferred by him to the acting-committee.

The principal officers of these societies were not fanatics; they were most eminent men in the land—judges of the courts, members of the Constitutional

VI. The treasurer shall pay all orders drawn by the president, or vice-president; which orders shall be his vouchers for his expenditures. He shall, before he enters on his office, give a bond of not less than 200*l.* for the faithful discharge of his duty.

VII. The duty of the councilors shall be to explain the laws and constitutions of the States, which relate to the emancipation of slaves; and to urge their claims to freedom, when legal, before such persons or courts as are authorized to decide upon them.

VIII. The electing-committee shall have sole power of admitting new members. Two-thirds of them shall be a quorum for this purpose; and the concurrence of a majority of them by ballot, when met, shall be necessary for the admission of a member. No member shall be admitted who has not been proposed at a general meeting of the Society; nor shall an election of a member take place in less than a month after the time of his being proposed. Foreigners, or other persons, who do not reside in this State, may be elected corresponding members of the Society without being subject to an annual payment, and shall be admitted to the meetings of the Society during their residence in the State.

IX. The acting-committee shall transact the business of the Society in its recess, and report the same at each quarterly meeting. They shall have a right, with the concurrence of the president or vice-president, to draw upon the treasurer for such sums of money as may be necessary to carry on the business of their appointment. Four of them shall be a quorum. After their first election, at each succeeding quarterly meeting, there shall be an election for two of their number.

Convention and of the Continental and United States Congress.

It is to be observed that there was no anti-slavery

X. Every member, upon his admission, shall subscribe the Constitution of the Society, and contribute ten shillings annually, in quarterly payments, towards defraying its contingent expenses. If he neglect to pay the same for more than six months, he shall, upon due notice being given him, cease to be a member.

XI. The Society shall meet on the first seventh-day, called Saturday, in the months called January, April, July, and October, at such time and place as shall be agreed to by a majority of the Society.

XII. No person, holding a slave as his property, shall be admitted a member of this Society; nevertheless, the Society may appoint persons of legal knowledge, owners of slaves, as honorary-counselors.

XIII. When an alteration in the Constitution is thought necessary, it shall be proposed at a previous meeting, before it shall take place. All questions shall be decided, where there is a division, by a majority of votes. In those cases where the Society is equally divided, the presiding officer shall have a casting vote.

OFFICERS OF THE SOCIETY.

President—PHILIP ROGERS.
Vice-President—JAMES CAREY.
Secretary—JOSEPH TOWNSEND.
Treasurer—DAVID BROWN.
Counselors—ZEBULON HOLLINGSWORTH, ARCHIBALD ROBINSON.
Honorary-Counselors—SAMUEL CHASE, LUTHER MARTIN.
Electing-Committee—JAMES OGLEBY, ISAAC GREIST, GEO. MATTHEWS, GEORGE PRESSTMAN, HENRY WILSON, JOHN BANKSON, ADAM FONER-

society in Massachusetts, which enjoys the reputation of originating all the radicalism of the land.* Slavery had come to an end there, about the year 1780; but when, or how, nobody is able to say definitely. Some even say that it was abolished there in 1776, by the Declaration of Independence declaring that "all men are created equal." Others claim that, substantially the same clause, "all men are born free and equal," incorporated into the declaration of rights in the State Constitution of 1780, abolished slavery. There was no action of the State Legislature on the subject, and no proclamation by the governor; yet it was as well settled in 1783, that there was no slavery in Massachusetts, as it is to-day. This came about by a decision of the Supreme Court that there was no slavery in the State, it being incompatible with the declaration of rights. "How, or by what act particularly," says Chief Justice Shaw, "slavery was abolished in Massachusetts, whether by the adoption of the opinion in Somerset's case as a

---

DEN, JAMES EICHELBERGER, WILLIAM HAWKINS, WILLIAM WILSON, THOMAS DICKSON, GER. HOPKINS.

Acting-Committee—JOHN BROWN, ELISHA TYSON, JAMES M'CANNON, ELIAS ELLICOTT, WILLIAM TRIMBLE, GEORGE DENT.

September 8, 1789.

*Of the one hundred and eighty-nine incorporators of the Rhode Island Society, one hundred and seventeen were from Rhode Island, sixty-eight from Massachusetts, three from Connecticut, and one from Vermont. The Nation, Nov. 28, 1872.

declaration and modification of the common law, or by the Declaration of Independence, or by the constitution of 1780, it is not now very easy to determine; it is rather a matter of curiosity than utility, it being agreed on all hands that, if not abolished before, it was by the declaration of rights." 18 Pickering, 209.*

*St. George Tucker, an eminent jurist, and Professor of Law at the College of William and Mary, at Williamsburg, Virginia, January 24, 1795, addressed a letter to Dr. Jeremy Belknap, of Boston, inquiring into the condition of the negroes in Massachusetts, and the circumstances under which slavery had come to an end in that state. His object was to obtain facts which he could use in removing prejudice against general emancipation in Virginia. "The introduction of slavery into this country," he says, "is at this day considered among its greatest misfortunes. I have cherished a hope that we may, from the example of our sister State, learn what methods are most likely to succeed in removing the same evils from among ourselves. With this view, I have taken the liberty to enclose a few queries, which, if your leisure will permit you to answer, you will confer on me a favor which I shall always consider as an obligation." He propounded eleven queries, to which Dr. Belknap replied at length. The correspondence is printed in the Massachusetts Historical Society's selections, iv, pp. 191–211. The next year Judge Tucker printed, at Philadelphia, his " Dissertation on Slavery, with a proposal for the gradual abolition of it in Virginia." Dr. Belknap's replies to Judge Tucker's inquiries have much historical interest. To the fifth query, " The mode by which slavery hath been abolished?" he says: " The general answer is, that slavery hath been abolished here by *public opinion*, which began to be established about thirty years ago. At the beginning of our controversy with Great Britain, several persons, who before had entertained sentiments opposed to the slavery of the blacks, did then take

Mr. Sumner asserted, in a speech in the Senate, June 28, 1854, that "in all her annals, no person was ever born a slave on the soil of Massachusetts." Mr. Palfrey, in his History of New England,* says: "In fact, no person was ever born into legal slavery in Massachusetts;" and Prof. Emory Washburn, in his Lecture, January 22, 1869, on "Slavery as it once prevailed in Massachusetts,"† says: "Nor does the fact that they were held as slaves, where the question as to their being such was never raised, militate with the

occasion publicly to remonstrate against the inconsistency of contending for their own liberty, and, at the same time, depriving other people of theirs. Pamphlets and newspaper essays appeared on the subject; it often entered into the conversation of reflecting people; and many who had, without remorse, been the purchasers of slaves, condemned themselves, and retracted their former opinion. The Quakers were zealous against slavery and the slave-trade; and by their means the writings of Anthony Benezet of Philadelphia, John Woolman of New Jersey, and others were spread through the country. Nathaniel Appleton and James Swan, merchants of Boston, and Dr. Benjamin Rush, of Philadelphia, distinguished themselves as writers on the side of liberty. Those on the other side generally concealed their names; but their arguments were not suffered to rest long without an answer. The controversy began about the year 1766, and was renewed at various times till 1773, when it was warmly agitated, and became a subject of forensic disputation at the public commencement at Harvard College." p. 201.

*Vol. ii, p. 30.

† Lectures by Members of the Mass. Historical Society on the Early History of Massachusetts, p. 216.

not in these states receive the same construction as in Massachusetts. In New Hampshire it was construed to mean that all persons *born* after 1784—the date of the adoption of the Constitution—were equally free and independent. In other words, it brought about gradual emancipation. In Virginia, it was simply a glittering generality—it had no legal meaning.*

In addition to the State Societies already named, there were several local societies in Virginia, Maryland, and Pennsylvania. All the abolition societies in the country were in correspondence and acted together. At the suggestion of the New York Society, a convention of delegates was called for the purpose of deliberating on the means of attaining their common object, and of uniting in a memorial to Congress. Delegates from ten of these societies, including the Virginia, Maryland,

---

*Dr. Belknap says the clause " all men are born free and equal " was inserted in the Declaration of Rights of Massachusetts " not merely as a moral and political truth, but with a particular view to establish the liberation of the negroes on a general principle, and so it was understood by the people at large; but some doubted whether it was sufficient "—p. 203. That some persons had this result in view is probable; but contemporaneous records and acts of the citizens do not justify the statement that " so it was understood by the people at large." Dr. Belknap was living in New Hampshire at the time, and did not come to Boston till 1786. The construction put upon the clause, by the Supreme Court, was evidently a happy afterthought; and was inspired by that *public opinion* to which Dr. Belknap himself, in his reply to Judge Tucker, ascribes the extinction of slavery.

position already stated—that no child was ever born into *lawful* bondage in Massachusetts, from the year 1641 to the present hour."

These statements, in substance the same, seem like a technical evasion. Thousands were born into actual slavery—whether it were legal or not was poor consolation to the slave—lived as slaves, were sold as slaves, and died as slaves in Massachusetts. They never knew they were freemen. The number of slaves in Massachusetts in 1776 was 5,249, about half of whom were owned in Boston, which had then a population of 17,500. The proportion of slaves to the whole population of Boston in 1776, was six times as great as the number of colored persons in Cincinnati to-day is to the whole population, and ten times as great as the present proportion of colored persons in Boston.*

The same declaration, that "all men are created equally free and independent," is found in the constitutions of New Hampshire and Virginia; but it did

---

*Mr. George H. Moore, in his elaborate work, "Notes on the History of Slavery in Massachusetts," expresses a doubt whether slavery legally came to an end in Massachusetts at the period stated above; and perhaps not before the adoption of the fourteenth amendment to the Constitution. He says: "It would not be the least remarkable of the circumstances connected with this strange and eventful history, that though *virtually* abolished before, the actual prohibition of slavery in Massachusetts, as well as Kentucky, should be accomplished by the votes of South Carolina and Georgia." p. 242.

Delaware, Pennsylvania, New Jersey, New York, Connecticut, and Rhode Island State Societies, and two local societies on the eastern shore of Maryland, met on the first day of January, 1794, at the Select Council Chamber in Philadelphia,* and drew up a joint memorial to Congress, asking for a law making the use of vessels and men in the slave trade a penal offense. Such a law was passed by Congress without debate.† These societies held annual conventions for many years. The convention recommended that such meetings of

---

*The Pennsylvanian Society assumed all the expenses of the Convention, of entertaining the delegates, and of printing the proceedings. The delegates of the Pennsylvanian Society were William Rogers, Samuel P. Griffiths, Samuel Coats, William Rawle, Robert Patterson, and Benjamin Rush. The printed proceedings of this convention, which is in the New York Historical Society's library, I have not had access to. Joseph Bloomfield, of New Jersey, an officer of the Revolution, attorney-general, governor of the state from 1801–12, and member of Congress from 1817–21, was president of the Convention.

†The memorial was presented in both branches of Congress, January 28, 1794. The record in the House was as follows: "A memorial from the several societies formed in different parts of the United States, for promoting the abolition of slavery, in convention assembled at Philadelphia, on the first instant, was presented to the House and read, praying that Congress may adopt such measures as may be the most effectual and expedient for the abolition of the slave-trade. Also, a memorial of the Providence Society, for abolishing the slave-trade, to the same effect. *Ordered,* That the said memorials be referred to Mr. Trumbull [of Connecticut], Mr. Ward [of Massachusetts], Mr. Giles

delegates be annually convened; that annual or periodical discourses or orations be delivered in public on slavery and the means of its abolition, in order that, "by the frequent application of the force of reason and the persuasive power of eloquence, slaveholders and their abettors may be awakened to a sense of their injustice, and be startled with horror at the enormity of their conduct."

The convention also adopted an address "To the citizens of the United States," which was drawn up by Dr. Benjamin Rush.*

[of Virginia], Mr. Talbot [of New York], and Mr. Grove [of North Carolina]; that they do examine the matter thereof, and report the same, with their opinion thereupon, to the House." Annals of Congress, iv, p. 349.

A bill was reported in conformity to the wishes of the memorialists, passed its several stages without debate, and was approved March 22, 1794. For the bill, see Id., p. 1426.

*The address is as follows:

"*To the Citizens of the United States:*

"The Address of the Delegates from the several Societies formed in different parts of the United States, for promoting the Abolition of Slavery, in convention assembled at Philadelphia, on the first day of January, 1794.

"FRIENDS AND FELLOW-CITIZENS: United to you by the ties of citizenship, and partakers with you in the blessings of a free government, we take the liberty of addressing you upon a subject highly interesting to the credit and prosperity of the United States.

"It is the glory of our country to have originated a system of opposition to the commerce in that part of our fellow-creatures who compose

Similar societies were formed in London and Paris, with whom these societies were in constant correspondence. Pennsylvania passed an act of gradual emancipation in 1780, and Rhode Island and Connecticut in 1784. A similar act, making all children born thereafter free, did not pass the Legislature of New York till 1799. In the meantime these societies were pouring in their memorials to State Legislatures and Congress, holding meetings, distributing documents, and rousing public sentiment to the enormities of the slave system.

The Connecticut petitioners say: "From a sober

---

the nations of Africa. Much has been done by the citizens of some of the States to abolish this disgraceful traffic, and to improve the condition of those unhappy people whom the ignorance, or the avarice of our ancestors had bequeathed to us as slaves. But the evil still continues, and our country is yet disgraced by laws and practices which level the creature man with a part of the brute creation. Many reasons concur in persuading us to abolish domestic slavery in our country. It is inconsistent with the safety of the liberties of the United States. Freedom and slavery can not long exist together. An unlimited power over the time, labor, and posterity of our fellow-creatures, necessarily unfits man for discharging the public and private duties of citizens of a republic. It is inconsistent with sound policy, in exposing the States which permit it, to all those evils which insurrections and the most resentful war have introduced into one of the richest islands in the West Indies. It is unfriendly to the present exertions of the inhabitants of Europe in favor of liberty. What people will advocate freedom, with a zeal proportioned to its blessings, while they view the purest republic in the world tolerating in its bosom a body of slaves? In vain has the tyranny of kings been rejected, while

conviction of the unrighteousness of slavery, your petitioners have long beheld with grief our fellow-men doomed to perpetual bondage in a country which boasts of her freedom. Your petitioners are fully of opinion that calm reflection will at last convince the world that the whole system of American slavery is unjust in its nature, impolitic in its principles, and in its consequences ruinous to the industry and enterprise of the citizens of these states."

we permit in our country a domestic despotism which involves in its nature most of the vices and miseries that we have endeavored to avoid. It is degrading to our rank as men in the scale of being. Let us use our reason and social affections for the purposes for which they were given, or cease to boast a pre-eminence over animals that are unpolluted by our crimes.

"But higher motives to justice and humanity towards our fellow-creatures, remain yet to be mentioned. Domestic slavery is repugnant to the principles of Christianity. It prostrates every benevolent and just principle of action in the human heart. It is rebellion against the authority of a common Father. It is a practical denial of the extent and efficacy of the death of a common Saviour. It is an usurpation of the prerogative of the Great Sovereign of the universe, who has solemnly claimed an exclusive property in the souls of men. But if this view of the enormity of the evil of domestic slavery should not affect us, there is one consideration more, which ought to alarm and impress us, especially at the present juncture. It is a violation of a Divine precept of universal justice, which has in no instance escaped with impunity. The crimes of nations, as well as individuals, are often designated in their punishments; and we conceive it to be no forced construction of some of the calamities which now distress or impend over our country,

The Virginia Society, petitioning Congress, says: "Your memorialists, fully aware that righteousness exalteth a nation, and that slavery is not only an odious degradation, but an outrageous violation of one of the most essential rights of human nature, and utterly repugnant to the precepts of the gospel, which breathes 'peace on earth and good will to men,' lament that a practice so inconsistent with true policy and the inalienable rights of men should subsist in so enlightened an age, and among a people professing to believe that they are the measure of the evils which we have meted to others. The ravages committed upon many of our fellow-citizens by the Indians, and the depredations upon the liberty and commerce of others, of the citizens of the United States by the Algerines, both unite in proclaiming to us in the most forcible language, 'to loose the bands of wickedness, to break every yoke, to undo the heavy burthens, and to let the oppressed go free.'

"We shall conclude this address by recommending to you:

"*First.* To refrain immediately from that species of rapine and murder which has improperly been softened by the name of the African trade. It is Indian cruelty and Algerine piracy in another form.

"*Second.* To form Societies in every State, for the purpose of promoting the abolition of the slave trade, of domestic slavery, for the relief of persons unlawfully held in bondage, and for the improvement of the condition of Africans and their desendants amongst us.

"The Societies which we represent, have beheld with triumph the success of their exertions in many instances, in favor of their African brethren; and, in full reliance upon the continuance of Divine support and direction, they humbly hope their labors will never cease while there exists a single slave in the United States."

that all mankind are, by nature, equally entitled to freedom."

The Pennsylvania Society memorialized Congress thus: "The memorial respectfully showeth: That from a regard for the happiness of mankind, an association was formed several years since in this state, by a number of her citizens of various religious denominations, for promoting the abolition of slavery, and for the relief of those unlawfully held in bondage. A just and acute conception of the true principles of liberty, as it spread through the land, produced accessories to their numbers, many friends to their cause, and a legislative co-operation with their views, which, by the blessing of Divine Providence, have been successfully directed to the relieving from bondage a large number of their fellow-creatures of the African race. They have also the satisfaction to observe that in consequence of that spirit of philanthropy and genuine liberty, which is generally diffusing its beneficial influence, similar institutions are forming at home and abroad.

"That mankind are all formed by the same Almighty Being, alike objects of his care and equally designed for the enjoyment of happiness, the Christian religion teaches us to believe, and the political creed of Americans fully coincides with the position.

"Your memorialists, particularly engaged in attending to the distresses arising from slavery, believe it their indispensable duty to present the subject to your notice.

They have observed with real satisfaction, that many important and salutary powers are vested in you for 'promoting the welfare and securing the blessings of liberty to the people of the United States;' and as they conceive that these blessings ought rightfully to be administered without distinction of color to all descriptions of people, so they indulge themselves in the pleasing expectation that nothing which can be done for the relief of the unhappy objects of their care will be either omitted or delayed."

"From a persuasion that equal liberty was originally the portion, and is still the birthright of all men, and influenced by the strong ties of humanity and the principles of their institution, your memorialists conceive themselves bound to use all justifiable endeavors to loosen the bands of slavery, and promote a general enjoyment of the blessings of freedom. Under these impressions they earnestly entreat your serious attention to the subject of slavery; that you will be pleased to countenance the restoration to liberty of those unhappy men, who, alone, in this land of freedom, are degraded into perpetual bondage; and who, amidst the general joy of surrounding freemen, are groaning in servile subjection; that you will devise means for removing this inconsistency from the character of the American people; and that you will step to the very verge of the power vested in you for discouraging every species of traffic in the persons of our fellow-men." Annals of Congress, i, p. 1239.

This memorial was drawn up and signed by " BENJAMIN FRANKLIN, *President*, Feb. 3, 1790." It was the last public act of that eminent man. He died on the 17th day of the April following. It will be observed that the memorial strikes at slavery itself, on the ground that the institution is unjust, and a national disgrace. It was so understood in Congress, and ruffled the equanimity of the representatives of South Carolina and Georgia. Mr. Jackson, of Georgia, distinguished himself in the debate by an elaborate defense of the institution. He was especially annoyed that Dr. Franklin's name should be attached to the memorial, "a man," he said, "who ought to have known the constitution better."*

---

* Mr. Jackson opposed the reference of the memorial to a committee, and wished it to be thrown aside. Mr. Burke, of South Carolina, said he saw the disposition of the House, and feared the memorial would be referred. He " was certain the commitment would sound an alarm, and blow the trumpet of sedition in the Southern States."

Mr. Seney, of Maryland, denied that there was anything unconstitutional in the memorial; its only object was that Congress should exercise their constitutional authority to abate the horrors of slavery as far as they could.

Mr. Parker, of Virginia, said : " I hope the petition of these respectable people will be attended to with all the readiness the importance of its object demands ; and I can not help expressing the pleasure I feel in finding so considerable a part of the community attending to

Dr. Franklin, though confined to his chamber, and suffering under a most painful disease, could not allow the occasion to pass without indulging his humor at the expense of Mr. Jackson. He wrote to the editor of the *Federal Gazette*, March 23, 1790, as follows: "Read-

matters of such momentous concern to the future prosperity and happiness of the people of America. I think it my duty as a citizen of the Union to espouse their cause."

Mr. Page, of Virginia (governor from 1802–1805), said he was in favor of the commitment. He hoped that the designs of the respectable memorialists would not be stopped at the threshold, in order to preclude a fair discussion of the prayer of the memorial. With respect to the alarm that was apprehended, he conjectured there was none; but there might be just cause, if the memorial was *not* taken into consideration. He placed himself in the case of a slave, and said that, on hearing that Congress had refused to listen to the decent suggestions of a respectable part of the community, he should infer that the general government (from which was expected great good would result to every class of citizens) had shut their ears against the voice of humanity; and he should despair of any alleviation of the miseries he and his posterity had in prospect. If anything could induce him to rebel, it must be a stroke like this. But if he was told that application was made in his behalf, and that Congress was willing to hear what could be urged in favor of discouraging the practice of importing his fellow-wretches, he would trust in their justice and humanity, and wait for the decision patiently. He presumed that these unfortunate people would reason in the same way.

Mr. Madison, of Virginia, said, if there were the slighest tendency by the commitment to break in upon the constitution, he would object to it; but he did not see upon what ground such an event could be apprehended. He admitted that Congress was restricted by the consti-

ing, last night, in your excellent paper, the speech of Mr. Jackson, in Congress, against their meddling with the affair of slavery, or attempting to mend the condition of the slaves, it put me in mind of a similar one made about one hundred years since by Sidi Mehemet Ibrahim, a member of the Divan of Algiers, which may be seen in Martin's Account of his Consulship, anno 1687. It was against granting the petition of a sect called *Erika*, or Purists, who prayed for the abolition of piracy and slavery as being unjust. Mr. Jackson does not quote it; perhaps he has not seen it. If, therefore, some of its reasonings are to be found in his eloquent speech, it may only show that men's interests and intel-

tution from taking measures to abolish the slave-trade; yet there was a variety of ways by which it could countenance the abolition of slavery; and regulations might be made in relation to the introduction of slaves into the new States, to be formed out of the Western Territory.

The memorial was committed by a vote of 43 yeas to 14 nays. Of the Virginia delegation, 8 voted yea and 2 nay; Maryland, 3 yea, 1 nay; Delaware and North Carolina, both delegations absent. Mr. Vining, the member for Delaware, however, spoke and voted later with the friends of the memorialists.

The committee reported on the 8th of March. The report was discussed in committee of the whole, and amended to read as follows:

"*First.* That the migration or importation of such persons as any of the States now existing shall think proper to admit, can not be prohibited by Congress prior to the year 1808.

"*Second.* That Congress have no authority to interfere in the emancipation of slaves, or in the treatment of them, in any of the States—

lects operate, and are operated on, with surprising similarity, in all countries and climates, whenever they are under similar circumstances. The African's speech, as translated, is as follows." He then goes on to make an ingenious parody of Mr. Jackson's speech, making this African Mussulman give the same religious, and other reasons, for not releasing the white Christian slaves, whom they had captured by piracy, that Mr. Jackson had made for not releasing African slaves.* There were inquiries in the libraries for "Martin's Account of his Consulship," but it was never found. The paper may be read in the second volume of Franklin's Works,

---

it remaining with the several States alone, to provide any regulations therein which humanity and true policy may require.

"*Third.* That Congress have authority to restrain the citizens of the United States from carrying on the African trade, for the purpose of supplying foreigners with slaves, and of providing, by proper regulations, for the humane treatment during their passage of slaves imported by the said citizens into the States admitting such importation."

This was the first legislation on the subject of slavery in the new Congress, and was carried by 29 votes to 25—North Carolina, South Carolina, and Georgia voting unanimously in the negative. All the other States (except Rhode Island, from which no member was present) voted in the affirmative or divided. New Hampshire voted 1 yea, 1 nay; Massachusetts, 6 yeas, 3 nays; Connecticut, 2 yeas, 2 nays; New York, 5 yeas, 2 nays; New Jersey, 3 yeas; Pennsylvania, 5 yeas; Virginia, 5 yeas, 6 nays; Maryland, 1 yea, 4 nays; Delaware, 1 yea.

*At this period, one hundred and fifteen American citizens, captured by piracy, were held as slaves in Algiers, for whom large ransoms were demanded by the pirates.

Sparks' edition, p. 518. None of Dr. Franklin's writings are more felicitous than this *jeu d' esprit;* and it was written only twenty-four days before his death.

In the midst of this period, when anti-slavery opinions were so generally held by leading statesmen, the Constitution of the United States was formed. It is due to the framers of that instrument to state that the entire delegations from the Northern and Middle States, and a majority of those from Virginia, Maryland, and Delaware were inspired to a greater or less extent with these sentiments, and would have supported any practical measures that would, in a reasonable time, have put an end to slavery. South Carolina and Georgia positively refused to come into the Union unless the clause, denying to Congress the power to prohibit the importation of slaves prior to 1808, was inserted. The Northern States were not so strenuous in opposition to this clause as Virginia and Maryland.* State after state was

---

*The convention, after discussing principles, appointed a "committee of detail," consisting of Mr. Rutledge of South Carolina, Mr. Randolph of Virginia, Mr. Wilson of Pennsylvania, Mr. Ellsworth of Connecticut, and Mr. Gorham of Massachusetts, to reduce to the form of a constitution the resolutions agreed upon. This committee without instructions, or authority from the resolutions adopted, introduced a clause forever prohibiting the abolition of the African slave-trade. Mr. Randolph earnestly protested against this clause. He was opposed to any restriction on the power of Congress to abolish it. He "could never agree to the clause as it stands. He would sooner risk the Constitution." Madison Papers, p. 1396. Mr. Ellsworth "was for leav-

abolishing the institution; anti-slavery opinions were becoming universal; and it was generally supposed at the North that slavery would soon die out. The financial and business interests of the country were prostrated. Union at any cost must be had. The words *slave* and *slavery* were carefully avoided in the draft, and the best terms possible were made for South Carolina and Georgia. The Constitution, as finally adopted, suited nobody; and by the narrowest margins it escaped being rejected in all the States. The vote in the Massachusetts Convention was 187 yeas to 168 nays; and in the Virginia Convention, 89 yeas to 78 nays.

From this examination of the subject, we see that the popular idea, that the political anti-slavery agitation was forced upon the South by the North, and especially by Massachusetts, is not a correct one. In the second period of excited controversy, from 1820 to 1830, the

---

ing the clause as it now stands. Let every State import what it pleases. The morality, the wisdom of slavery, are considerations belonging to the States themselves. What enriches a part, enriches the whole; and the States are the best judges of their particular interest." Id., p. 1389. It was moved, as a compromise, to guarantee the slave-trade for twenty years, by postponing the restriction to 1808. This motion was seconded by Mr. Gorham, of Massachusetts, and it passed. Mr. Madison, of Virginia, opposed it. "Twenty years," he said, "will produce all the mischief that can be apprehended from the liberty to import slaves. So long a term will be more dishonorable to the American character, than to say nothing about it in the Constitution." Id., p. 1427. Mr. Mason, of Virginia, pronounced the traffic as "infernal." Id., p. 1390.

South again took the lead. In 1827, there were one hundred and thirty abolition societies in the United States. Of these one hundred and six were in the slaveholding States, and only four in New England and New York. Of these societies eight were in Virginia, eleven in Maryland, two in Delaware, two in the District of Columbia, eight in Kentucky, twenty-five in Tennessee, with a membership of one thousand, and fifty in North Carolina, with a membership of three thousand persons.* Many of these societies were the result of the personal labors of Benjamin Lundy.

The Southampton insurrection of 1830, and indications of insurrection in North Carolina the same year, swept away these societies and their visible results. The fifteen years from 1830 to 1845 were the darkest period the American slave ever saw. It was the reign of violence and mob law at the North. This was the second great reaction. The first commenced with the invention of the cotton-gin, by Eli Whitney, in 1793, and continued till the question of the admission of Missouri came up in 1820. The third reaction was a failure; it commenced in 1861, and resulted in the overthrow of the institution.

---

*Life of Benjamin Lundy, Phil. 1847, p. 218. The total membership of the 130 societies was 6625, exclusive of twelve societies in Illinois from which no returns had been received. These statistics were gathered by the American Anti-Slavery Convention, which was held at Philadelphia, in 1827.

In the year 1791, the date that Dr. Buchanan delivered his oration at Baltimore, the College of William and Mary, in Virginia, conferred upon Granville Sharp, the great abolition agitator of England, the degree of LL. D. Granville Sharp had no other reputation than his anti-slavery record. This slender straw shows significantly the current of public opinion in Virginia at that time. If Granville Sharp had come over some years later to visit the President and Fellows of the College which had conferred upon him so distinguished an honor, it might have been at the risk of personal liberty, if not of life.

Colleges are naturally conservative, both from principle and from policy. Harvard College has never conferred upon Wm. Lloyd Garrison the least of its academic honors. Wendell Phillips, its own alumnus, the most eloquent of its living orators, and having in his veins a strain of the best blood of Boston, has always been snubbed at the literary and festive gatherings of the College. Southern gentlemen, however, agitators of the divine and biblical origin of slavery, have ever found a welcome on those occasions, for which latter courtesy the College should be honored.

If the visitor who records his name in the register of the Massachusetts Historical Society, will turn to the first leaf, he will find standing at the head the autograph of Jefferson Davis. Whether this position of honor was assigned by intention, or occurred accidentally, I can not state. But there it is, and if you forget to look for yourself, it will probably be shown to you by the attendant.

Mr. Davis, with his family, visited Boston in 1858, and was received with marked attention by all. During this visit he was introduced, and frequently came to the Athenæum, where I made his acquaintance. Among other objects of interest in the institution, I showed him Washington's library and this oration of Dr. Buchanan. Nothing so fixed his attention as this; he read it and expressed himself amazed. He had heard that such sentiments were expressed at the South, but had never seen them.

I am conscious that while I have taxed your patience, I have given but an imperfect presentation of the subject. If this endeavor shall serve to incite members of the Club to investigate the subject for themselves, my object will have been attained.

Addenda.

Since the preceding pages were in type, I have seen, in the library of the New York Historical Society, the printed minutes of the first convention held by the Abolition Societies of the United States, which met at Philadelphia, January 1, 1794, and was several days in session, of which mention was made on page 59. These minutes show that my statement of the societies represented needs correction. The Rhode Island Society appears to have had no delegates present. The Virginia Society appointed delegates; but, for reasons stated below, they were not admitted. Several societies, however, were represented, of which before I had seen no mention. As the convention met in the depth of winter, and as traveling was then expensive and difficult, it is evidence of a deep interest in the subject, that so many delegations attended.

The convention met in the City Hall, at Philadelphia, and organized by choosing Joseph Bloomfield, of New Jersey, President; John McCrea, Secretary; and Joseph Fry, Door-keeper.

The following societies were represented by the delegates named:

Connecticut Society—Uriah Tracy.

New York Society—Peter Jay Munroe, Moses Rogers, Thomas Franklin, Jr., William Dunlap.

New Jersey Society—Joseph Bloomfield, William Coxe, Jr., John Wistar, Robert Pearson, Franklin Davenport.

Pennsylvania Society—William Rogers, William Rawle, Samuel Powel Griffitts, Robert Patterson, Samuel Coates, Benjamin Rush.

Washington (Pa.) Society—Absalom Baird.

Delaware Society—Warren Mifflin, Isaiah Rowland, Joseph Hodgson, John Pemberton.

Wilmington (Del.) Society—Joseph Warner, Isaac H. Starr, Robert Coram.

Maryland Society—Samuel Sterett, James Winchester, Joseph Townsend, Adam Fonerdon, Jesse Hollingsworth.

Chester-town (Md.) Society—Joseph Wilkinson, James Maslin, Abraham Ridgely.

A letter, directed to the convention, from Robert Pleasants, chairman of the Committee of Correspondence of the Virginia Society, was presented and read. By this letter it appeared that Samuel Pleasants and Israel Pleasants, of Philadelphia, were appointed to represent that society in the convention; and in case of their declining, or being prevented from acting, the convention were at liberty to nominate two other persons as their representatives. In the letter was inclosed "an authentic account of several vessels lately fitted out in Virginia for the African slave-trade." The convention, after considering the proposition of the Virginia Society, adopted the following resolution:

"*Resolved*, That as information, and an unreserved comparison of one another's sentiments, relative to the important cause in which we are severally engaged, are our principal objects; and as the persons appointed by the Virginia Society are not citizens of that State, nor members of that Society, to admit them, or, according to their proposal, for us to elect others as their representatives, would be highly improper."

The president was directed to acknowledge the receipt of the letter, to inform the Virginia Society of the above resolution, and to thank them for the important information contained in the letter.

Benjamin Rush, William Dunlap, Samuel Sterett, William Rawle, and Warner Mifflin, were appointed a committee to report the objects proper for the consideration of the convention, and the best plan for carrying the same into execution. Under the direction of this committee, memorials were prepared to be sent to the legislatures of the several States which had not abolished slavery; a memorial to Congress asking for the enactment of a law making the use of vessels and men in the slave-trade a penal offense; and an address to the citizens of the United States, already printed in a note, pp. 60–63. It was also voted " to recommend to the different Abolition societies to appoint delegates to meet in convention, at Philadelphia, on the first Wednesday of January, 1795, and on the same day in every year afterward, until the great objects of their original association be accomplished."

I was so fortunate as to find, also, in the New York Historical Society's library, the minutes of the conventions of 1795 and 1797. The convention of 1795 met in the City Hall, at Philadelphia, January 7, and continued in session till the 14th of that month. The societies represented, and delegates, were as follows:

Rhode Island Society—Theodore Foster. The credentials from the president of the society stated that George Benson was also appointed to represent the society; but he did not appear.

Connecticut Society—Jonathan Edwards, Uriah Tracy, Zephaniah Swift.

New York Society—John Murray, Jr., William Johnson, Lawrence Embree, William Dunlap, William Walton Woolsey.

New Jersey Society—James Sloan, Franklin Davenport. Other delegates appointed, Joseph Bloomfield, William Coxe, Jr., and John Wistar, did not appear. It was explained to the convention that the absence of Mr. Bloomfield was occasioned by sickness.

Pennsylvania Society—William Rawle, Robert Patterson, Benjamin Rush, Samuel Coates, Caspar Wistar, James Todd, Benjamin Say.

Washington (Pa.) Society—Thomas Scott, Absalom Baird, Samuel Clark.

Delaware Society—Richard Bassett, John Ralston, Allen McLane, Caleb Boyer.

Wilmington (Del.) Society—Cyrus Newlin, James A. Bayard, Joseph Warner, William Poole.

Maryland Society—Samuel Sterett, Adam Fonerdon, Joseph Townsend, Joseph Thornburgh, George Buchanan, John Bankson, Philip Moore.

Chester-town (Md.) Society—Edward Scott, James Houston.

Dr. Benjamin Rush was elected President; Walter Franklin, Secretary; and Joseph Fry, Door-keeper.

Jonathan Edwards, William Dunlap, Caspar Wistar, Cyrus Newlin, Caleb Boyer, Philip Moore, and James Houston were appointed the committee on business. Memorials were prepared, and adopted by the convention, to be sent to the legislatures of South Carolina and Georgia, as both States still persisted in the importation of slaves. An address to the Abolition Societies of the United States was also adopted, the spirit of which may be inferred from the following extract:

"When we have broken his chains, and restored the African to the enjoyment of his rights, the great work of justice and benevolence is not accomplished. The new-born citizen must receive that instruction, and those powerful impressions of moral and religious truths, which will render him capable and desirous of fulfilling the various duties he owes to himself and to his country. By educating some in the higher branches, and all in the useful parts of learning, and in the precepts of religion and morality, we shall not only do away the reproach and calumny so unjustly lavished upon us, but confound the enemies of truth, by evincing that the unhappy sons of Africa, in spite of the degrading influence of slavery, are in nowise inferior to the more fortunate inhabitants of Europe and America."

The fourth annual convention of the Abolition Societies of the United States was held in the Senate Chamber, at Philadelphia, May 3, 1797. The societies represented, and delegates, were as follows:

New York Society—Willett Seaman, Thomas Eddy, Samuel L. Mitchell, William Dunlap, Elihu Hubbard Smith.

New Jersey Society—Joseph Bloomfield, Richard Hartshorne, Joseph Sloan, William Coxe, Jr., William Carpenter.

Pennsylvania Society—Benjamin Rush, William Rawle, Samuel P. Griffitts, Casper Wistar, Samuel Coates, Robert Patterson, James Todd.

Maryland Society—Francis Johonnett, Jesse Tyson, Gerrard T. Hopkins.

Choptank (Md.) Society—Seth Hill Evitts.

Virginia Society (at Richmond)—Joseph Anthony.

Alexandria (Va.) Society—George Drinker.

Joseph Bloomfield was elected President; Thomas P. Cope, Secretary; and Jacob Meyer, Door-keeper.

Communications from the New York, New Jersey, Pennsylvania, Maryland, Choptank (Md.), Virginia, and Alexandria (Va.) Abolition Societies were read. The minutes of the convention of 1797 are more elaborately compiled, and contain more statistics than the previous reports. Among other papers adopted by the convention, was an "Address to the Free Africans." Besides the seven societies, which sent delegates, the eight societies following, which sent none, were reported, viz: the Rhode Island, Connecticut, Washington (Pa.), Delaware (at Dover), Wilmington (Del.), Chester-town (Md.), Winchester (Va.), and Kentucky Societies. Among the memorials presented to Congress, in 1791, was one from the Caroline County (Md.) Society. Besides the Maryland Society, at Baltimore, there appear to have been three local societies on the Eastern Shore of that State.

The several societies reported their membership, in 1797, as follows: New York Society, two hundred and fifty; New Jersey Society, "compiled partially;" Pennsylvania Society, five hundred and ninety-one; Maryland Society, two hundred and thirty-one; Choptank (Md.) Society, twenty-five; Wilmington (Del.) Society, sixty; Virginia Society, one hundred and forty-seven; Alexandria (Va.) Society, sixty-two. From the other societies no reports of membership were received. The Choptank (Md.) Society, formed in 1790, reported having liberated more than sixty slaves; the Wilmington (Del.) Society reported having liberated eighty since 1788; and the Alexandria (Va.) Society reported having made twenty-six complaints under the law against the importation of slaves. By votes of previous conventions, the Abolition Societies were required to sustain schools for the education of Africans. The minutes for 1797 contain interesting reports from the several societies of their success in this department of benevolence.

Before the year 1782, it was illegal in Virginia for a master to liberate his slaves without sending them out of the State. The Assembly of Virginia then passed an act permitting the manumission of slaves. Judge Tucker, of that State, in his "Dissertation on Slavery," estimated that, from 1782 to 1791, ten thousand slaves were liberated in Virginia by their masters.

Of the anti-slavery literature of this period, which has not already been noticed, there is in the New York Historical Society's library, "An Oration spoken before the Connecticut Society for the Promotion of Freedom, and the Relief of Persons unlawfully held in Bondage, convened at Hartford the 8th of May, 1794. By Theodore Dwight.* Hartford, 1794." 8vo, 24 pp. Also, a "Discourse delivered April 12, 1797, at the Request of the New York Society for Promoting the Manumission of Slaves, and protecting such of them as have been or

---

*The "Dwight" to whom, with others, Bishop Grégoire inscribed his "Literature of Negroes," was probably Theodore Dwight, and not President Timothy Dwight, as stated on page 31.

·may be liberated. By Samuel Miller, A. M. New York, 1787." 8vo, 36 pp.

In the Boston Athenæum library are the following tracts:

"A Dissuasion to Great Britain and the Colonies from the Slave Trade to Africa. By James Swan. Revised and abridged. Boston, 1773." 8vo, 40 pp. The original edition was printed in 1772.

"A Forensic Dispute on the Legality of Enslaving the Africans, held at a Public Commencement in Cambridge, N. E., July 21, 1773, by the Candidates for the Bachelors' Degrees. Boston, 1773." 8vo, 48 pp.

"A Short Account of that Part of Africa inhabited by the Negroes. [By Anthony Benezet.] Philadelphia, 1772." 8vo, 80 pp.

"An Address to the British Settlements in America upon Slaveholding. Second edition. To which are added Observations on a Pamphlet entitled 'Slavery not forbidden by Scripture; or, a Defence of the West Indian Planters.' By a Pennsylvanian [Dr. Benjamin Rush]. Philadelphia, 1773." 8vo, pp. 28 + 54. Also, another edition issued the same year, with the title somewhat varied; the second part being termed, "A Vindication of the Address to the Inhabitants," etc. The pamphlet entitled "Slavery not forbidden by Scripture," etc., was written by R. Nisbet, and is in the Library of Congress.

" Memorials presented to the Congress of the United States, by the different Societies instituted for promoting the Abolition of Slavery, in the States of Rhode Island, Connecticut, New York, Pennsylvania, Maryland, and Virginia. Published by the Pennsylvania Society for promoting the Abolition of Slavery. Philadelphia. Printed by Francis Bailey, 1792." 8vo, 31 pp.

This tract contains the memorials which were presented to the House of Representatives, December 8, 1791, and which were read and referred. The Rhode Island memorial is signed by David Howell, President, and dated December 28, 1790. Connecticut—by Ezra Stiles, President; Simon Baldwin, Secretary; January 7, 1791. New York—by Matthew Clarkson, Vice-President; December 14, 1790.

Pennsylvania—by James Pemberton, President; John McCrea and Joseph P. Norris, Secretaries; October 3, 1791. Washington (Pa.)—by Andrew Swearingen, Vice-President. Maryland, in Baltimore—" Signed by the members generally;" but the names of no members are given. Chester-town, Maryland—by James M. Anderson, President; Daniel McCurtin, Secretary; November 19, 1791. Caroline County, Maryland—by Edward White, Vice-President; Charles Emery, Secretary; September 6, 1791.

Of the sixteen Abolition Societies existing in the United States during this decade, it appears that six were in States which, at the outbreak of the late rebellion, were non-slaveholding; and ten were in slaveholding States.

DR. GEORGE BUCHANAN'S
ORATION ON SLAVERY,
BALTIMORE, July 4, 1791.

AN

ORATION

UPON THE

MORAL AND POLITICAL EVIL

OF

SLAVERY.

DELIVERED AT A PUBLIC MEETING

OF THE

MARYLAND SOCIETY

FOR PROMOTING THE

ABOLITION of SLAVERY,

And the RELIEF of *FREE NEGROES*, and others unlawfully held in BONDAGE.

BALTIMORE, July 4th, 1791.

By GEORGE BUCHANAN, M. D.
Member of the *American Philosophical Society.*

BALTIMORE: Printed by PHILIP EDWARDS.
M,DCC,XCIII.

* * * * * * * * * * * * * * * * * * * *

At a special meeting of the "MARYLAND SOCIETY *for promoting the Abolition of Slavery, and the Relief of free Negroes and others unlawfully held in Bondage,*" held at Baltimore, *July* 4*th*, 1791,—
 "UNANIMOUSLY RESOLVED

THAT the President present the Thanks of this Society to Dr. *George Buchanan,* for the excellent ORATION, by him delivered this Day—and at the same time request a copy thereof in the Name and for the Use of the Society."

Extract from the Minutes.
JOSEPH TOWNSEND, Secretary.

President, SAMUEL STERETT,
Vice President, ALEX^R. M'KIM.

* * * * * * * * * * * * * * * * * * *

To the Honorable
THOMAS JEFFERSON, Esq.
SECRETARY OF STATE,

WHOSE Patriotism, since the American Revolution, has been uniformly marked, by a sincere, steady and active Attachment to the Interest of his Country; and whose literary Abilities have distinguished him amongst the first of Statesmen and Philosophers—

THIS ORATION

Is respectfully inscribed, as an humble Testimony of the highest Regard and Esteem, by

The AUTHOR.

ORATION

CITIZENS *and* FELLOW-MEMBERS,

SUMMONED by your voice, I appear before you with diffidence; the arduous task you have imposed upon me, would have been better executed by some one of greater abilities and information, and one more versed in public speaking.

However, my feeble exertions shall not be wanting to promote the intentions of so laudable an institution; and while I endeavour to fulfil the purport of this meeting, I shall hope not to fail in proving its utility.

Too much cannot be offered against the unnatural custom that pervades the greatest part of the world, of dragging the human race into slavery and bondage, nor of exposing the ignominy of such barbarity.

Let an impartial view of man be taken, so far as it respects his existence, and in the chain of thought, the *white*, *swarthy* and *black*, will be all linked together, and at once point out their equality. God hath created mankind after his own image, and granted to them liberty and independence; and if varieties may be found in their structure and colour, these are only to be attributed to the nature of their diet and habits, as also of the soil and climate they may inhabit, and serve as flimsy pretexts for enslaving them.

In the first rudiment of society, when simplicity characterised the conduct of man, slavery was unknown, every one equally enjoyed that peace and tranquility at home, to which he was naturally born: But this equality existed but for a time; as yet no laws, no government was established to check the ambitious, or to curb the crafty; hence reprisals were made upon the best property by the strong and robust, and finally subjected the weak and indigent to poverty and want.

Here then arose a difference in the circumstances of men, and the poor and weak were obliged to submit themselves to the control of the rich and powerful; but although the authority exercised was at first mild, and ensured to the bondsmen almost the same privileges with their masters, yet the idea of power soon crept in upon the mind, and at length lenity was converted into rigidity, and the gall of servitude became insupportable; the oppressed, soon found that *that liberty*, which they had just given up, was an inalienable privilege of man, and sought means to regain it: this was effected,—but not until a time when ignorance began to decline, when improvements were made in the arts, commerce and governments, and when men could seek protection from law, or by industry could ward off the bitterness of poverty, and ensure to themselves an independence.

Happy circumstance! To feel oneself emancipated from the chains of slavery, must awaken every delicate sensation of the soul, and transport the gloomy mind into a region of bliss; for what is life, without an enjoyment of those privileges which have been given to us by nature? It is a burden, which, if not awed by Divine Providence, would be speedily cast off, by all who sweat under the yoke of slavish servitude, and know no alternative but an unceasing submission to the goads of a brutal master.

Ages have revolved since this happy condition of human affairs; and although mankind have been gradually verging from a state of simplicity to a more social refinement, yet the governments of those primitive times laid open an analogy for licentiousness; and we find, by pursuing the history of man, that slavery was again introduced, and stained the annals of all the powers of Europe.

The idea of possessing, as property, was too lucrative to be totally eradicated; it diffused itself into Egypt and Cyprus, which became the first and most noted markets for the sale and purchase of slaves, and soon became the cause of rapine and bloodshed in Greece and Rome: there it was an established custom to subject to slavery all the captives in time of war; and not only the Emperors, but the nobility, were in possession of thousands—to them they served as instruments of diversion and authority.

To give an idea only of the amphitheatrical entertainments, so repugnant to humanity, would make the most obdurate heart feel with keen sensibility. For to hear with patience of
voracious

voracious animals being turned loose among human beings, to give sport to the rich and great, when, upon reflection, he may be assured, that the merciless jaw knew no restraint but precipitately charged upon its prey whom it left, without remorse, either massacred or maimed.

Such was the practice among the ancients, and to charge the modern with like enormities, would by many be deemed criminal.

But I fear not to accuse them—the prosecution of the present barbarous and iniquitous slave trade affords us too many instances of cruelties exercised against the harmless Africans. A trade, which, after it was abolished in Europe by the general introduction of Christianity, was again renewed about the fourteenth century by the mercenary Portuguese, and now prosecuted by the Spaniards, French and British, in defiance of every principle of justice, humanity and religion.

Ye moderns, will you not blush at degenerating into ancient barbarity, and at wearing the garb of Christians, when you pursue the practices of savages?

Hasten to reform, and put an end to this unnatural and destructive trade—Do you not know that thousands of your fellow-mortals are annually entombed by it? and that it proves ruinous to your government? You go to Africa to purchase slaves for foreign markets, and lose the advantages of all the proper articles of commerce, which that country affords. You bury your seamen upon the pestiferous shores; and, shocking to humanity! make monsters of all you engage in the traffic.

Who are more brutal than the Captains of vessels in the slave trade? Not even the tawny savage of the American wilds, who thirsts after the blood of the Christian, and carries off his scalp the trophy of splendid victory!

They even countenance the practice of the ancients, in seeing a sturdy mastiff tear in pieces some poor wretch of their hateful cargoes, or in viewing their wreathes and tortures, when smarting under the lash of a seasoned cat.*

It is time to abolish these enormities, and to stay such repeated insults from being offered to Divine Providence: Some dreadful curse from heaven may be the effect of them, and the innocent be made to suffer for the guilty.

What, will you not consider that the Africans are men? that they have human souls to be saved? that they are born free and independent? A violation of which prerogatives is an infringement upon the laws of God.

But

A whip with nine tails.

But, are these the only crimes you are guilty of in pursuing the trade? No—you stir up the harmless Africans to war, and stain their fields with blood: you keep constant hostile ferment in their territories, in order to procure captives for your uses; some you purchase with a few trifling articles, and waft to distant shores to be made the instruments of grandeur, pride and luxury.

You commit also the crime of kidnapping others, whom you forcibly drag from their beloved country, from the bosoms of their dearest relatives; so leave a wife without a husband, a sister without a brother, and a helpless infant to bemoan the loss of its indulgent parent.

Could you but see the agonizing pangs of these distressed mortals, in the hour of their captivity, when deprived of every thing that is dear to them, it would make even the heathenish heart to melt with sorrow; like a noble Senator of old, death is their choice in preference to lingering out their lives in ignominious slavery—and often do we see them meet it with a smile.

The horrors of the grave intimidate not even the delicate females; too many melancholy instances are recorded of their plunging into the deep, and carrying with them a tender infant at the breast; even in my own recollection, suicide has been committed in various forms by these unhappy wretches, under the blind infatuation of revisiting the land of their nativity.

Possessed of Christian sentiments, they fail not to exercise them when an opportunity offers. Things pleasing rejoice them, and melancholy circumstances pall their appetites for amusements.— They brook no insults, and are equally prone to forgiveness as to resentment; they have gratitude also, and will even expose their own lives, to wipe off the obligation of past favours; nor do they want any of the refinements of taste, so much the boast of those who call themselves Christians.

The talent for music, both vocal and instrumental, appears natural to them: Neither is their genius for literature to be despised; many instances are recorded of men of eminence amongst them: Witness Ignatius Sancho, whose letters are admired by all men of taste—Phillis Wheatley, who distinguished herself as a poetess—The physician of New Orleans—The Virginia calculator—Banneker, the Maryland Astronomer, and many others whom it would be needless to mention. These are sufficient to shew, that the Africans, whom you despise, whom you inhumanly treat as brutes, and whom you unlawfully subject to slavery, with the tyrannizing hands of Despots, are equally capable of improvements with yourselves.

This

This you may think a bold assertion, but it is not made without reflection, nor independent of the testimony of many, who have taken pains with their education.

Because you see few, in comparison to their number, who make any exertions of abilities at all, you are ready to enjoy the common opinion, that they are an inferior set of beings, and destined by nature to the cruelties and hardships you impose upon them.

But be cautious how long you hold such sentiments; the time may come, when you will be obliged to abandon them—consider the pitiable situation of these most distressed beings; deprived of their liberty and reduced to slavery; consider also, that they toil not for themselves, from the rising of the Sun to its going down, and you will readily conceive the cause of their inaction.

What time, or what incitement has a slave to become wise? there is no great art in hilling corn, or in running a furrow; and to do this, they know they are doomed, whether they seek into the mysteries of science, or remain ignorant as they are.

To deprive a man of his liberty, has a tendency to rob his soul of every spring to virtuous actions; and were slaves to become fiends, the wonder could not be great. Nothing more assimilates a man to a beast, says the learned Montesque, than being among freemen, himself a slave; for slavery clogs the mind, perverts the moral faculty, and reduces the conduct of man to the standard of brutes.

What right then have you to expect greater things from these poor mortals? You would not blame a brute for committing ravages upon his prey, nor ought you to censure a slave, for making attempts to regain his liberty even at the risque of life itself.

Ye mercenary Portuguese, ye ambitious French, and ye deceitful Britons, I again call upon you to take these things into your consideration; it is time, a remorse of conscience had seized upon you; it is time, you were apprised of your danger: Behold the thousands that are annually lost to your governments, in the prosecution of an unlawful and iniquitous trade.

View the depredations that you commit upon a nation, born equally free with yourselves; consider the abyss of misery into which you plunge your fellow-mortals, and reflect upon the horrid crimes you are hourly committing under the bright sunshine of revealed religion.—Will you not then find yourselves upon a precipice, and protected from ruin, only because you are too wicked to be lost?

What

What Empire, or what State can have the hope of existing, which prosecutes a trade, that proves a sinking fund to her coffers, and to her subjects, that tramples the human species under foot, with as much indifference as the dirt, and fills the world with misery and woe?

Let not a blind hardness of opinion any longer bias your judgments, and prevent you from acting like Christians.

View the Empires amongst the ancients; behold Egypt in the time of Secostris, Greece in the time of Cyrus, and Rome in the reign of Augustus; view them all, powerful as enemies, patterns of virtue and science, bold and intrepid in war, free and independent; and now see them sacrificed at the shrine of luxury, and dwindled into insignificance. When in power, they usurped the authority of God, they stretched out their arms to encompass their enemies, and bound their captives in iron chains of slavery.

Vengeance was then inflicted, their spoils became the instruments of pride, luxury and dissipation, and finally proved the cause of their present downfall.

Then look back at home; view your degeneracy from the times of Louis the 14th and Charles the 2d, and if a universal blush don't prevail, it will argue a hardness of heart, tempered by a constant action of wickedness upon the smooth anvil of religion.

For such are the effects of subjecting man to slavery, that it destroys every human principle, vitiates the mind, instills ideas of unlawful cruelties, and eventually subverts the springs of government.

What a distressing scene is here before us. America, I start at your situation! The idea of these direful effects of slavery demand your most serious attention.—What! shall a people, who flew to arms with the valour of Roman Citizens, when encroachments were made upon their liberties, by the invasion of foreign powers, now basely descend to cherish the seed and propagate the growth of the evil, which they boldly sought to eradicate. To the eternal infamy of our country, this will be handed down to posterity, written in the blood of African innocence.

If your forefathers have been degenerate enough to introduce slavery into your country, to contaminate the minds of her citizens, you ought to have the virtue of extirpating it.

Emancipated from the shackles of despotism, you know no superior; free and independent, you stand equally respected among your

your foes, and your allies.—Renowned in history, for your valour, and for your wisdom, your way is left open to the highest eminence of human perfection.

But while with pleasing hopes you may anticipate such an event, the echo of expiring freedom cannot fail to assail the ears, and pierce the heart with keen reproach.

In the first struggles for American freedom, in the enthusiastic ardour for attaining liberty and independence, one of the most noble sentiments that ever adorned the human breast, was loudly proclaimed in all her councils—

Deeply penetrated with a sense of *Equality*, they held it as a fixed principle, "*that all men are by nature and of right ought to be free, that they are created equal and endowed by their Creator with certain inalienable rights, amongst which are life, liberty and the pursuit of happiness.*"

Nevertheless, *when* the blessings of peace were showered upon them, *when* they had obtained these rights which they had so boldly contended for, *then* they became apostates to their principles, and rivetted the fetters of slavery upon the unfortunate Africans.

Deceitful men! who could have suggested, that American patriotism would at this day countenance a conduct so inconsistent; that while America boasts of being a land of freedom, and an asylum for the oppressed of Europe, she should at the same time foster an abominable nursery for slaves, to check the shoots of her growing liberty?

Deaf to the clamours of criticism, she feels no remorse, and blindly pursues the object of her destruction; she encourages the propagation of vice, and suffers her youth to be reared in the habits of cruelty.

Not even the sobs and groans of injured innocence, which *reek* from every State, can excite her pity, nor human misery bend her heart to sympathy.

Cruel and oppressive she wantonly abuses the *Rights of Man*, and willingly sacrifices her liberty at the altar of slavery: What an opportunity is here given for triumph among her enemies? Will they not exclaim, that upon this very day, while the Americans celebrate the anniversary of Freedom and Independence, abject slavery exists in all her States but one.*

How degenerately base to merit the rebuke. Fellow-countrymen, let the heart of humanity awake and direct your counsels;
reflect

*Massachusetts.

reflect that slavery gains root among you; look back upon the curses which it has heaped upon your ancestors, and unanimously combine to drive the *fiend Monster* from your territories; it is inconsistent with the principles of your government, with the education of your youth, and highly derogatory to the true spirit of Christianity.

In despotic governments, says Montesque, where they are already in a state of political slavery, civil slavery is more tolerable than in other governments; for there the minds of masters and servants are equally degenerate and act in unison.—But in America, this cannot be the case; here the pure forms of Republicanism are established, and hold forth to the world the enjoyment of Freedom and Independence.

Her citizens have thrown off the load of oppression, under which they formerly laboured; and elated with their signal victories, have become oppressors in their turn.

They have slaves, over whom they carry the iron rod of subjection, and fail not to exercise it with cruelty, hence their situations become insupportable, misery inhabits their cabins, and persecution pursues them in the field.

I would wish to be partial to my country, and carry a hand of lenity; it is more pleasing to celebrate than to detract, but whoever takes a view of the situation of its slaves, will find it even worse than this description.

Naked and starved, they often fall victims to the inclemencies of the weather, and inhumanly beaten; sacrifices to the turbulent tempers of their cruel masters.

Unfortunate Africans! born in freedom, and subjected to slavery! How long will you remain the spoils of despotism, and the harbinger of human calamities? Cannot your distresses awaken the heart of sensibility, and excite her pity? Cannot your unlawful treatment call forth the voice of humanity to plead your cause?

Americans! step forward; you have already diffused a spirit of Liberty throughout the world; you have set examples of heroism; and now let me intreat you to pave the way to the exercise of humanity: an opportunity is offered to raise yourselves to the first eminence among mankind.

Rouse then from your lethargy, and let not such torpid indifference prevail in your councils.—Slavery, the most implacable enemy to your country, is harboured amongst you; it makes a rapid progress, and threatens you with destruction.

Already

Already has it disturbed the limpid streams of liberty, it has polluted the minds of your youth, sown the seeds of despotism, and without a speedy check to her ravages, will sink you into a pit of infamy, where you shall be robbed of all the honours you have before acquired.

Let it be viewed either morally or politically, and no one argument can be adduced in its favour.

The savage mind may perhaps become reconciled to it, but the heart of the Christian must recoil at the idea.—He sees it forbidden in Holy Writ, and his conscience dictates to him, that it is wrong.

"*He that stealeth a man,*" says Exodus, "*and selleth him, or if he be found in his hand, he shall surely be put to death.*"

Oh my countrymen! are there any of you who can con over this elegant passage of Scripture, without trembling; or can you stand before the great Author of your existence, with an arm uplifted to subject his creatures to slavery, without dreading an execution of this divine threat.

"*The nation, to whom they shall be in bondage, will I judge, said God*"—and what that judgment may be, is beyond the suggestion of mortals. We may be hurled amidst the elements of woe to expiate the guilt, for he who holdeth men in slavery liveth in sin.

In a civilized country, where religion is tolerated in all its purity, it must be the fault of ignorance, or a stubborn indifference to Christianity, to rebel against divine sentiments; and considering slavery in a political view, it must appear equally as destructive to our terrestial happiness, as it endangers our enjoyment of heavenly bliss.

For who is there, unless innured to savage cruelties, that can hear of the inhuman punishments daily inflicted upon the unfortunate Blacks, without feeling for their situations?

Can a man who calls himself a Christian, coolly and deliberately tie up, thumb screw, torture with pincers, and beat unmercifully a poor slave, for perhaps a trifling neglect of duty? Or can any one be an eye witness to such enormities, without at the same time being deeply pursuaded of its guilt?

I fear these questions may be answered in the affirmative, but I hope by none of this respectable audience; for such men must be monsters, not of the regular order of nature, and equally prone to murder, or to less cruelties.

But independent of these effects, which the existence of slavery in any country has over the moral faculty of man, it is highly injurious to its natural œconomy; it debars the progress of agriculture, and gives origin to sloth and luxury.

View the fertile fields of Great Britain, where the hand of freedom conducts the plowshare, then look back upon your own, and see how mean will be the comparison.

Your labourers are slaves, and they have no inducement, no incentive to be industrious; they are cloathed and victualled, whether lazy or hard-working; and from the calculations that have been made, one freeman is worth almost two slaves in the field, which makes it in many instances cheaper to have hirelings; for they are incited to industry by the hopes of reputation and future employment, and are careful of their apparel and their instruments of husbandry, where they must provide them for themselves, whereas, the others have little or no temptation to attend to any of these circumstances.

But this, the prejudiced mind is scarce able to scan, the pride of holding men as property is too flattering to yield to the dictates of reason, and blindly pushes on man to his destruction.

What a pity is it, that darkness should so obscure us, that America with all her transcending glory, should be stigmatized with the infamous reproach of oppression, and her citizens be called Tyrants.

Fellow-countrymen, let the hand of persecution be no longer raised against you.—Act virtuously; do unto all men as you would they should do unto you, and exterminate the pest of slavery from your land.

Then will the tongues of slander be silenced, the shafts of criticism blunted, and America enter upon a new theatre of glory.

But unless these things shall be done, unless the calamitous situation of the slaves shall at least be alleviated, what is America to expect? Can she think that such repeated insults to Divine Authority will pass off with impunity? Or can she suppose, that men, who are naturally born free, shall forever sweat under the yoke of ignominious slavery, without making one effort to regain their liberty?

No, my countrymen, these things are not to be expected.— Heaven will not overlook such enormities! She is bound to punish impenitent sinners, and her wrath is to be dreaded by all! Moreover, the number of slaves, that are harboured amongst you holds forth an alarm; in many parts of the continent they exceed the whites, and are capable of ransacking the country.

What

What then, if the fire of Liberty shall be kindled amongst them? What, if some enthusiast in their cause shall beat to arms, and call them to the standard of freedom? Would they fly in clouds, until their numbers became tremendous, and threaten the country with devastation and ruin?—It would not be the feeble efforts of an undisciplined people, that could quell their fury.

Led on by the hopes of freedom, and animated by the aspiring voice of their leader, they would soon find, that "a day, an hour of virtuous liberty, was worth a whole eternity of bondage."

Hark! Methinks I hear the work begun, the Blacks have sought for Allies, and found them in the wilderness; they have called the rusty savages to their assistance, and are preparing to take revenge of their haughty masters.*

A revenge, which they consider as justly merited; for being no longer able to endure their unnatural and unlawful bondage, they are determined to seek Liberty or Death.

Why then is there not some step to be taken to ward off the dreadful catastrophe?

Fellow countrymen, will you stand and see your aged parents, your loving wives, your dutiful children butchered by the merciless hand of the enthusiast, when you have it in your power to prevent it?

In this enlightened period, when the Rights of Man is the topick of political controversy, and slavery is considered not only unnatural but unlawful, why do you not step forward and compleat the glorious work you have begun, and extend the merciful hand to the unfortunate Blacks? Why do you not form some wise plan to liberate them, and abolish slavery in your country?

If it should be deemed injudicious or impolitic to effect it at once, let it be done gradually; let the children for one or two generations be liberated at a certain age, and in less than half a century will the plague be totally rooted out from amongst you—then will you begin to see your consequence—thousands of good citizens will be added to your number, and your arms will become invincible: Gratitude will induce *them* to become your friends; for the PROMISE alone of freedom to a slave ensures his loyalty; witness their conduct in the second Punic war which the Senate of Rome carried on against Hannibal; not a man
disgraced

---

*This was thrown out as a conjecture of what possibly might happen, and the insurrections in St. Domingo tend to prove the danger, to be more considerable than has generally been supposed, and sufficient to alarm the inhabitants of these States.

disgraced himself, but all with an intrepidity peculiar to veterans, met their foes, fought and conquered.

Witness also the valour of a few Blacks in South-Carolina, who under the promise of freedom, joined the great and good Colonel JOHN LAURENS; and in a sudden surprised the British, and distinguished themselves as heroes.

I remember it was said, they were foremost in the ranks, and nobly contended for their promised reward.

At this critical juncture, when savage cruelties threatened to invade your peaceful territories, and murder your citizens, what great advantage might be derived from giving freedom to the Africans at once. Would they not all become your Allies; would they not turn out hardy for the wilderness, to drive the blood-thirsty savage to his den, and teach him it were better to live peceably at home, than to come under the scourge of such newly liberated levies.

Americans arouse—It is time to hear the cause of the wretched sons of Africa, enslaved in your country; they plead not guilty to every charge of crime, and unmeritedly endure the sufferings you impose upon them.

Yet, like haughty Despots, or corrupt judges, you forbid a trial. Justice however to yourselves and humanity toward your fellow mortals, loudly demand it of you, and you ought not to hesitáte in obeying their sacred mandates.

A few years may be sufficient to make you repent of your unrelenting indifference, and give a stab to all your boasted honours; then may you, pitiable citizens, be taught wisdom, when it will be too late; then may you cry out, Abba Father, but mercy will not be found, where mercy was refused.

Let all the social feelings of the soul, let honour, philanthropy, pity, humanity, and justice, unite to effect their emancipation.

For eternal will be the disgrace of keeping them much longer in the iron fetters of slavery, but immortal the honour of accomplishing their FREEDOM.

To the SOCIETY.

SUCH were the sentiments, my friends, that first induced you to form yourselves into this Society.

For seeing human nature debased in the most vile manner, and
seeing

seeing also that your country deeply suffered from the iniquitous custom of holding man in slavery, you have justly concluded " that at this particular crisis, when Europe and America appear to pay some attention to this evil, the united endeavours of a few, might greatly influence the public opinion, and produce from the transient sentiment of the times, effects, extensive, lasting and useful."—But however great have been your exertions; however much they have been guided by the precepts of humanity and religion, your public reward has been censure and criticism; but let not such airy weapons damp your ardour for doing good; your *just reward* is in Heaven, not on earth.

Yours is the businesss of mercy and compassion, not of oppression. You forcibly rescue from the hands of no man his property, but by your examples and precepts you promote the Abolition of Slavery, and give relief to free Negroes, and others unlawfully held in bondage.

You have shown an anxiety to extend a portion of that freedom to others, which GOD in his Providence hath extended unto you, and a release from that thraldom to which yourselves and your country were so lately tyrannically doomed, and from which you have been but recently delivered. You have evinced to the world your inclination to remove as much as possible the sorrows of those who have lived in undeserved bondage, and that your hearts are expanded with kindness toward men of all colours, conditions and nations; and if you did not interest yourselves in their behalf, how long might their situations remain hard and distressing.

Numbers might passively remain for life in abject slavery from an ignorance of the mode of acquiring their emancipation, notwithstanding they may be justly entitled to their freedom by birth and by the law.

If the hand of prosecution is now raised against you, for relieving your fellow mortals from the distresses of unlawful slavery, and restoring them to liberty, it is to be hoped it will not be of long duration; the principles of your institutions will be daily made more known, and others will begin to think as you do; they will find upon reflection, that they have no just power or authority to hold men in slavery, and seeing that your actions are charitable and disinterested, will cordially inlist under your banners, and aid your benevolent exertions.

Already have you reason to suppose, that your good examples have been influencial; you humbly began with a few, and you now see your numbers hourly encreasing.

It may be the effusions of a youthful fancy, solicitous of aggrandizing your merit, but I fear not to say, that the operations of similar institutions will date one of the most splendid æras of American greatness.

Go on then, my friends, pursue the dictates of an unsullied conscience, and cease not until you have finished your work—but let prudence guide you in all your undertakings, and let not an enthusiastic heat predominate over reason. Your cause is a just one, consistent with law and equity, and must finally be advocated by all men of Humanity and Religion.

" For, 'tis Liberty alone which gives the flower
" of fleeting life its lustre and perfume,
" And we are weeds without it."
TASK.

FINIS.